ELSTREE AERODROME
90 YEARS IN PICTURES

GRANT PEERLESS AND RICHARD RIDING

Title page photograph: Elstree Aerodrome. *(Pete Stevens)*

First published 2003; this updated edition first published 2024

The History Press
97 St George's Place, Cheltenham,
Gloucestershire, GL50 3QB
www.thehistorypress.co.uk

© Richard Riding & Grant Peerless, 2003, 2024

The right of Richard Riding & Grant Peerless to be identified as the Authors of this work has been asserted in accordance with the Copyright, Designs and Patents Act 1988.

All rights reserved. No part of this book may be reprinted or reproduced or utilised in any form or by any electronic, mechanical or other means, now known or hereafter invented, including photocopying and recording, or in any information storage or retrieval system, without the permission in writing from the Publishers.

British Library Cataloguing in Publication Data.
A catalogue record for this book is available from the British Library.

ISBN 978 1 80399 598 4

Typesetting and origination by The History Press
Printed and bound in Great Britain by TJ Books Limited, Padstow, Cornwall

Authors' notes

There has been no attempt to include in this book a photograph of every aircraft ever based at Elstree, or the procession of thousands of visiting aircraft that have touched down over the years. This would have necessitated a 20-volume series, at least, and would probably have resulted in the ultimate, if expensive, cure for insomnia! As my father and I took most of the photographs this is very much a personal selection but hopefully it gives the true flavour of Elstree from its postwar revival to more recent times. During the last thirty years or so the resident Elstree aircraft population has been dominated by Cessna and Piper 'spamcans' from across the Atlantic, a poor reflection if nothing else on the failed postwar British light aircraft industry. Where they have been included they are more often than not the first examples of their type to appear on the British civil aircraft register.

Frustratingly, because we have found only one pre-war photograph taken at Aldenham/Elstree aerodrome, we have had to make do with photographs of specific aircraft based, but not photographed at Elstree during this period. Should any reader come across a hoard of pre-war photographs the authors would be delighted to see them! Initial contact should be made via the publishers, please.

Richard Riding

When I took early retirement in 1999 from a career in civil engineering I wanted something totally different to occupy my time. It did not take me long to find the answer. I had been visiting Elstree Aerodrome on and off since the mid-1950s, when I used to cycle there from my home in St Albans, a mammoth journey of at least eight miles! It struck me that very little had been written about the aerodrome, unlike other nearby airfields of Hatfield, Radlett, Bovingdon, etc. and I decided to research the history of Elstree. I was particularly interested in its pre-war connections with a country club and curious about any wartime activity.

I set about the task and a year or so later had a paper published in *Airfield Review*, the house journal of the Airfield Research Group, of which I am a member. An abbreviated version appeared in *Hertfordshire Countryside* magazine and this is when I first came across my co-author. I needed some more photographs to illustrate my article and by coincidence Richard Riding had recently written a piece in *Wingspan* which featured a selection of his father's excellent pictures of the Halifax operation at Elstree. I contacted the publishers of *Wingspan* who put me in touch with Richard – I could not believe my luck when I discovered that he also lived in St Albans. It transpired that Richard had himself been intending to write the history of Elstree and had accumulated a lot of information but had not got around to putting pen to paper. He suggested that we got together and collaborated on a book, which would bring together my research and the vast collection of photographs taken by him and his father over a period of more than fifty years. The result is this book.

Grant Peerless

Contents

Foreword to the 2024 Edition   5
Introduction to the 2024 Edition   6
Foreword by John Houlder CBE DSc   7
Introduction by Richard Riding   9

1 Pre-War Beginnings   13
2 'Ubend'um, Wemend'um'   23
3 Postwar Heavyweights and Lightweights   41
4 Years of Peace   59
5 Elstree in the Twenty-first Century   65
6 Private Residents   73
7 Giving Them Wings   95
8 For Business and Pleasure   107
9 Rotary Club   135
10 Elstree Miscellany   141
11 Down in the Dumps   155
12 Prangs   159
13 People   167
14 Wolves in Sheep's Clothing   175
15 Pulling the Crowds   189

Significant Historical Events   194
Events Since 2003   195
Sources & Acknowledgements   224

To Marjorie Riding
Despite the tragic death in 1950 of her husband in an Auster flying from Elstree Aerodrome, without a single word of discouragement, my mother watched me embark upon a career in aerial photography flying in Austers based at Elstree.

Richard Riding

E.J. 'Eddie' Riding (1916–1950).

Life has been likened to a game of snakes and ladders. The late John 'Tubby' Simpson, Colonel H.C. Butcher DSO and Keith Ewart provided the rungs that gave the opportunities that have resulted in this book.

Foreword to the 2024 Edition

Thanks to the legendary tenure of John Houlder CBE, DSc, which spanned three generations of our family, we had little involvement in Elstree Aerodrome for nearly sixty years of its ninety-year life. From 1950, when John took on the lease from our great-grandfather, until his retirement in 2010, we relied on his passion for aviation and business to almost single-handedly reverse Elstree's waning fortunes and transform it into a popular post-war airfield, with a famous culture and some incredibly well-attended events in the 'good old days'.

My family has now had the joy of managing Elstree for over a decade, getting to know its many quirks and characters, working with our great team and customers, and making improvements where we can. We want to respect the past while looking to the future; preserve the aerodrome's heritage while upgrading its infrastructure and services; help our resident schools and businesses grow; and enable cleaner, quieter flight as technologies develop. We want Elstree to be a community asset with a fantastic range of amenities, events and educational initiatives, such as open days and the Air League's 'Soaring to Success' programme.

We are well aware of our status as the last licensed airfield in a county that has such rich aeronautical history, and we want to ensure that this standing grows long into the twenty-first century and beyond.

As well as John and many others, we are grateful to the late Richard Riding, without whose iconic images this book would not have been possible, and his co-author Grant Peerless, who has driven this new paperback edition twenty years after its original publication.

Humphrey Gibbs

Introduction to the 2024 Edition

I took early retirement in 1999 from a career in civil engineering and then worked as a consultant until retiring finally in 2013. After co-writing *Elstree Aerodrome: The Past in Pictures* with Richard Riding in 2003, we researched the history of nearby Leavesden Aerodrome and as a result *Leavesden Aerodrome: From Halifaxes to Hogwarts* was published in 2011.

I then began work on a long-held ambition to write a book about all the airfields in the British Isles, and *UK Airfields Past and Present: A Directory of Airfields from 1908 to 2018* was eventually published in 2020. I have also written numerous aviation-related articles for magazines and continue to do so.

In the summer of 2022 Humphrey Gibbs, Elstree Aerodrome operator, was making arrangements for an open day at the aerodrome and had enlisted the help of Mark Mockridge of nbalchemy to photograph the event. Having acquired a copy of my Elstree book, Humphrey contacted me to request my help with material for display boards setting out the brief history of the aerodrome. During the course of our discussions the idea to update *Elstree Aerodrome: The Past in Pictures* to coincide with the aerodrome's 90th anniversary in July 2024 was born. Mark was happy to provide the necessary photographs from his extensive collection taken at the aerodrome and Humphrey undertook to update events since he took on the management following the death of John Houlder. Mike Murphy, the aerodrome manager, also offered his assistance.

I continue to fly from Elstree with my pilot friend and have so far visited over 130 airfields all over England.

Sadly, my good friend and co-author Richard Riding passed away in January 2019 and this revised edition of the book is dedicated to him.

My thanks go to Humphrey, Mark and Mike for their invaluable contributions to this book. Also to Amy Rigg of The History Press for believing in the project.

Grant Peerless

Foreword

My recollection of how I became the tenant and operator of Elstree Aerodrome is as follows. I kept Miles Messenger G-AJOD at Elstree from 1948 onwards. London Aero & Motor Services (LAMS) were operating a flying school with three Austers but were mainly engaged in ferrying fruit from Italy in converted Halifax bombers. After one of these aircraft made a heavy landing and punched a hole in the extremely thin wartime concrete, tearing off its undercarriage and finishing up on the present site of the Cabair flying school, they decided to move to Stansted.

The Managing Director was Doc Humby and there was a large stock of Halifax spares at Stansted. He negotiated with the Ministry of Supply to buy these spares and told his fellow directors that, although the paperwork had not been completed, they now owned the spares and should help themselves. This they duly did, but

John Houlder with his Aero Commander 680E G-AWOE at Elstree in July 2003. *(RTR)*

they broke in at night because the watchman would not let them in by day. As a result they were prosecuted, the prosecution being based on their own statements, and sent to prison – all except Mr Simpson who made a classic remark which I think is equal to the famous 'Well, he would, wouldn't he?' of Mandy Rice-Davis. He said, 'I am not going to make a statement because I have nothing to make a statement about.'

The other person to escape jail was Doc Humby himself who was ill in hospital. He was tried later and found not guilty on grounds that he honestly believed that he had bought the spares. I have never understood how it is possible in law for staff to be imprisoned for carrying out a function when the jury later decided they genuinely believed the goods belonged to them.

The result was that I flew in to Elstree one Friday and found all the employees having a farewell party and they persuaded me to take on the management of the aerodrome and pay their wages for a few weeks to avoid them all being dispersed. With extreme reluctance I agreed and the next day, Saturday, went to see Lord Aldenham, the chairman of Westminster Bank, who was at his desk as usual. The result was an initial week-to-week agreement for the operation of the aerodrome which somehow has survived three generations of Lord Aldenhams.

This book should be of great interest to those who have come in contact with Elstree Aerodrome over the past fifty years.

Elstree is probably best remembered for the number of characters it has created – from Jeff Warne's voice on the radio to Jock Russell's dog, Haggis, which, on one occasion, had the whole front page of the *Daily Mirror* devoted to it, under the heading 'Plane bites dog'.

I have been managing Elstree Aerodrome for more than fifty years but even so Richard and Grant have dug out much history of which I was unaware. In some ways this is a social history of our times, which may be studied by historians a very long time in the future. I myself am very grateful for this book and the memories it is keeping for me.

John Houlder CBE DSc

Introduction

I was first taken to Elstree Aerodrome at the age of four, in 1946. My first ever flight was made from there on 14 April 1946 in Auster Autocrat G-AGXJ and to this day I recall my baptism of the air with some embarrassment. After I was strapped into the rear seat of the brand-new cream Auster the pilot, a chap called Forth, climbed into the left-hand seat, while my father, Eddie, strapped himself in beside him. There was an acrid smell of exhaust as the engine burst into life and the whole aircraft vibrated, as Austers do. As we taxied out to the runway it was just like being in a car. But the noise as the Cirrus Minor was opened to full power on take-off was not and frightened me half to death. Worse was to come. As I looked out of the window the ground, quite unexpectedly, dropped away and I watched in horror as the world below took on an entirely new and unnerving perspective. I wanted above

A never-to-be forgotten moment. Co-author Richard Riding was standing beside his father when this LAMS Halifax beat up Elstree several times during an air display on 27 July 1947. *(RTR)*

all else to get back down to earth but was trapped instead in a noisy cocoon divorced from reality with no means of escape. I must have made a noisy appeal to 'go down', for after a flight of less than five minutes duration we landed. In the remarks column of my father's flying logbook is the line 'Dick's 1st flight – emergency landing!' Ahem!

From 1946 until early 1950 my father and I were regular visitors to Elstree Aerodrome, it being only a short drive from our Hendon home. During this time my father worked for *Aeromodeller* magazine and in addition to designing and building flying scale models for the Aeromodeller Plans Service he wrote a series of articles on full-size aircraft, for which he produced high standard 1/72 scale drawings and provided his own photographs.

The dominating features at Elstree in the early postwar days were the blue LAMS Halifax freighters dispersed by the taxiway. Fitted with large belly panniers these aircraft were certificated and maintained at Elstree until the company moved its entire operation out to Stansted at the end of 1946. LAMS' chief engineer at Elstree was John 'Tubby' Simpson who, during the war, had worked with my father on Halifaxes being assembled and test-flown at nearby Leavesden. When LAMS moved out John set up Simpsons Aero Services at Elstree. Two other childhood memories of Elstree stick in my mind. At the age of five I attended the 1947 Elstree air display, when a BOAC Sandringham and one of the LAMS Halifaxes beat the place up, much to my joy and the rest of the 12,000-strong crowd. But I treasure most the memory of flying with my father in Piper Cub G-AKAA. He left learning to fly quite late, soloing in 'AA' in March 1949 at the age of 33. Sadly our trips together were all too few. On April 7 1950 he and aviation artist Stanley Orton Bradshaw took off from Elstree in Auster Autocar G-AJYM to cover the opening of the Boston Aero Club in Lincolnshire for *The Aeroplane*. On leaving Boston in the afternoon for the return flight to Elstree the Autocar, with Bradshaw at the controls, inexplicably spun in from about 700ft. Both men and a third occupant were killed instantly. Only a couple of days earlier I had flown in the Cub with my father, blissfully unaware that it would be my last flight with him. It would be another eight years before I was to see Elstree Aerodrome again.

After I left school in July 1958 I was determined to get into aviation, despite the circumstances under which I had lost my father. Useless at maths and science subjects I was unsuccessful in obtaining an apprenticeship at Handley Page at Cricklewood and with other aircraft companies elsewhere. During the Easter holiday that year an old friend of my father had taken me to Elstree. Understandably it was an emotional experience. Apart from the new reservoir adjacent to the western edge of the aerodrome the place had changed very little over eight years; even a few of the aircraft around in the late 1940s were still there. There was only one familiar face that I recognised – wrestling with something oily beneath an Auster in the main hangar was the unmistakable profile of 'Tubby' Simpson, complete with ubiquitous beret. After showing us around the hangar Tubby invited me to return after I had left school.

It was during this second visit to Elstree that Tubby Simpson offered me a summer job as a general dogsbody. I was only too pleased to clean aircraft and carry out tasks that nobody else seemed interested in doing. One of the first jobs I was given was to dispose of a Percival Proctor dumped behind the main hangar. Aircraft preservation was virtually unheard of in those days and with no conscience at all I eagerly set about the blameless aircraft with an axe. In time, and it took a hell of a long time, I reduced Mr Percival's pride and joy to manageable lumps for taking down to the dump at the end of the runway. Thus my first contribution to aviation had been totally destructive!

I landed my first real job quite by chance after chatting with a chap who worked on the opposite side of the main hangar. Michael White turned out to be the photographer for Derby Aerosurveys, an aerial photography outfit run by Derby Aviation, the company responsible for operating the flying school. Derby Aerosurveys just happened to have a vacancy for a darkroom lad and following an informal chat with the boss, an elderly retired lieutenant-colonel by the name of Butcher, I started work straight away. I took to the work easily but the novelty of processing someone else's films and prints soon wore off and I pleaded with Col Butcher to be let loose in one of the company's Austers with a camera. The chance came one spring evening. On April 10 1959 CFI Eddie Wild flew me in Auster Autocrat G-AGTP on a 30-minute trip round the local area. After landing I spent half the night processing and printing the results, so that a set of 12 x 10in prints would be on the boss's desk at 9 a.m. the following day. Col Butcher was impressed and before too long I was entrusted to carry out commissioned jobs up and down the country on my own. In 1960 Michael White, my mentor, left to join Meridian Airmaps and I was made chief, and only, photographer, aged just 18. Incidentally, the company's other Auster was G-AGXT, from which my late father took many aerial photographs in the late 1940s. This dream of a job continued for two more years until September 1962 when, no doubt unable to afford my salary of £3 15s a week, Derby Aerosurveys ceased trading! It looked as though it was goodbye to Elstree for a second time.

During my time at Elstree I had become friendly with TV commercial advertisement producer and private pilot Keith Ewart, who kept his Auster Aiglet G-AMMS there. On the day before I left Derby Aerosurveys he suggested that with his help and using his Aiglet as a camera-ship, I should carry on as a freelance. This arrangement worked well and I continued as a freelance aerial photographer until 1971, when I joined the editorial staff of *Flight International*. This led to my founding *Aeroplane Monthly* in April 1973, of which I was Editor until I took early retirement in 1998.

From the mid-1980s my visits to Elstree became less frequent and I see from my logbook that my last flight from there was made in July 1984. During my time working at Elstree during the 1950s and 1960s I made many lasting friendships, particularly with student pilots, many of whom later became airline captains and who are now mostly retired from commercial flying. Forty years later Elstree is still turning out pilots and has grown into one of the most popular and well-established general aviation aerodromes in Britain, despite its shortcomings.

It used to be said that anyone who learnt to fly at Elstree was capable of flying into almost anywhere. With its adjacent reservoir, electric power lines and relatively short runway new students and some visitors still find Elstree a little intimidating. It was more so in the early days before the use of radio, when the grass strip with its tricky approach over the pylons was in use and with Handley Page Victor bombers and Herald airliners from nearby Radlett aerodrome often in the circuit. Although the aerodromes at nearby Hatfield, Hendon, Leavesden and Radlett have since disappeared Elstree has somehow survived, despite the continual whingeing from generations of protesters on the grounds of noise. Today the aerodrome enjoys a relatively harmonious relationship with its neighbours even though it is sandwiched between four suburban towns.

Richard T. Riding
December 2003

An aerial view of Elstree Aerodrome, looking north-east, taken in the early 1970s. *(RTR)*

1 Pre-War Beginnings

It is generally accepted that Elstree Aerodrome in Hertfordshire has its origins in the Club that was based at Aldenham House. The house was built in the seventeenth century and had various owners until Henry Hucks Gibbs, the first Lord Aldenham, took up residence in 1868. He and his second son Vicary spent more than sixty years transforming the house into an opulent country retreat. They also acquired a magnificent collection of trees and plants to create one of the finest gardens in England, at one time employing more than ninety gardeners. After Vicary Gibb's death in 1932 the house stood empty for a year until it was leased to a syndicate headed by a Captain William Watkins, who converted it into a country club and residential health resort known as the Aldenham House Club. It opened in January

Aldenham House dates from the 1630s and is pictured here in 1934, the year in which it was converted into a country club and health resort. A landing ground for visiting members and their guests was opened on the opposite side of the road to the club in January 1934, but the site was not developed into a licensed aerodrome until later that year, when Aircraft Exchange & Mart Ltd moved in. Today Aldenham House is the administrative centre of Haberdashers' Aske's school, built from 1961 on adjacent land close to the eastern end of the runway. *(The Aeroplane)*

14 Elstree Aerodrome

1934 and soon became a playground for high society, boasting a polo field, nine-hole golf course, tennis and squash courts. A landing ground for visiting members and guests opened at the same time as the club but it is believed that an airstrip existed on the Aldenham Estate as early as 1930. Indeed, on 18 April 1933, No. 2 Tour of Sir Alan Cobham's National Aviation Day Display took place at Ham Farm, near Elstree, which was adjacent to the present aerodrome. Furthermore, Cobham had a habit of using airfields for his displays before they were officially opened. However, another report suggests that the venue was a mile away on a field to the east of the Watford bypass on the north side of Elstree Road, leading up to Aldenham Reservoir. Contemporary press reports are not specific about the location, 'Ham Farm', 'Elstree'

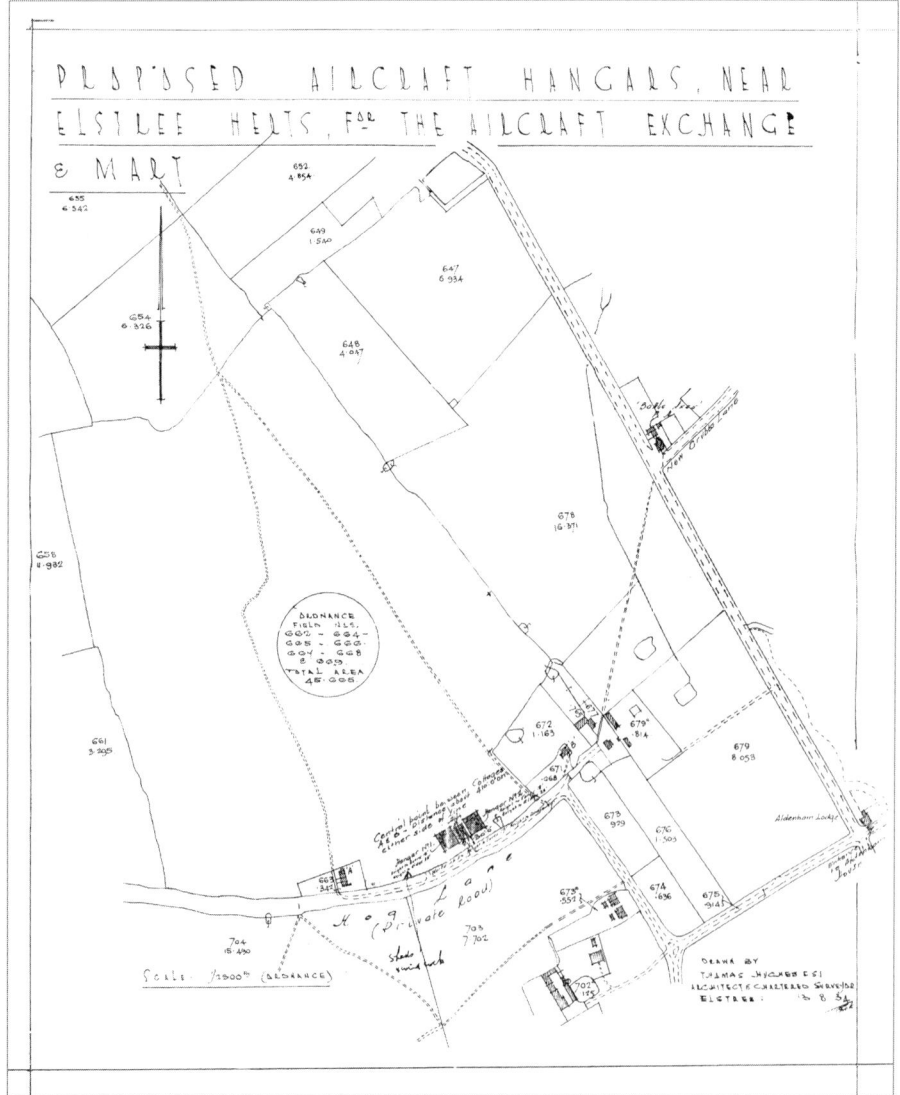

Dated 13 August 1934 and drawn to an original scale of 1/2500, this is the earliest known plan of Aldenham Aerodrome and shows the proposed hangars later built for Aircraft Exchange & Mart Ltd adjacent to Hog Lane, a private road. The Battle Axes public house can be seen midway along the road running diagonally at right, with Aldenham Lodge at the entrance to Aldenham House at bottom right.

and 'Aldenham' being the only clues. Prior to the 1933 event Sir Alan invited senior members of Elstree Parish Council to fly with him but they declined, preferring to 'stay down below'! The landing ground covered some 40 acres of Page's Farm, on the opposite side of the road from the club, and was also used by Lord Aldenham to exercise his thoroughbred horses. Facilities were minimal, consisting only of a petrol pump and a wooden hut containing a telephone. In the 1930s flying was considered smart and fashionable and many of the visiting polo players owned their own aircraft which they flew into the aerodrome, while other private pilots dropped in for lunch at the Club. Today the house is part of the Haberdashers' Aske's school complex. The aerodrome was known generally as Aldenham before and during the Second World War and Elstree after the war.

In April 1934 Captain Watkins applied to the Air Ministry for an aerodrome licence and this was duly granted on 28 July for a three-month period only. Interestingly, it was referred to as Elstree (Aldenham Lodge) on the licence, not Aldenham as it was commonly known at that time. An inspection by the Air Ministry on 19 September noted that the wooden frame of a hangar was under construction but that there were no other buildings on the site. Also, a chalk circle with the name 'Aldenham' in 10ft letters had been placed near the centre of the site. More importantly, the Inspector considered that the proximity of high tension cables and their attendant pylons rendered the site unsafe for flying instruction and therefore unsuitable for licensing as a permanent aerodrome. These cables were to prove a major obstacle to any expansion of the aerodrome in the future.

Use of the aerodrome was light until the autumn of 1934 when Aircraft Exchange & Mart, a private hire/charter/sales/service agent arrived on the scene. This came

This photograph of Avro 504N G-AEMP was taken in front of Aircraft Exchange & Mart's hangar at their headquarters at Hanworth Aerodrome, Middlesex. The company acquired premises at Aldenham in the autumn of 1934 and developed the site as a licensed aerodrome, remaining there until November 1939, when all civil flying in Britain ceased. (EJR)

Although this photograph was not taken at Aldenham it features the Spartan Arrow bought for £200 in August 1936 from Brian Lewis by Walter Mycroft, head of British International Pictures at Borehamwood near Elstree. Mycroft was disabled and had the controls of the Arrow specially modified so that he could handle the aircraft safely. The aircraft was sold to the Yapton Aero Club at Ford, Sussex, in August 1939. *(The Aeroplane)*

A visitor to Aldenham in 1936 was Lord Beaverbrook's silver and green DH90 Dragonfly G-AEHC. In July 1936 the aircraft was registered to London Express Newspapers Ltd and crashed in Newton Stewart, Wigtownshire on 2 February 1937. *(RTR Collection)*

about because Flt Lt Bernard J.W. Brady, the managing director, was a friend of Captain Watkins and a regular visitor to the Aldenham House Club. He was a former Royal Naval Air Service pilot and one of the pioneers of naval flying. The company's main base was at Hanworth where it operated as the London Air Park Flying Club, and it had other facilities on Guernsey and the Isle of Man, and at Croydon and Denham. It was agent for the Monospar, Blackburn B2 and Hendy Heck, as well as used aircraft. Aircraft Exchange & Mart was also agent for the Aeronca 100 which was built by the Aeronautical Corporation of Great Britain at Peterborough, where it shared a production line with engine manufacturers J.A. Prestwich Ltd (JAP).

The Air Ministry eventually issued a licence to Aircraft Exchange & Mart on 18 January 1935 but again only on a temporary basis for six months because of the inadequacies of the aerodrome. This covered only joyriding, taxi work and displays, but not instruction. The manager at Aldenham was Maj H.S. Shield, formerly of the Royal Flying Corps and a superb stunt pilot. Aircraft Exchange & Mart also ran the Watford & West Herts branch of the London Air Park Flying Club, otherwise known as the Aldenham Flying Club, from the aerodrome, with two DH60 Moths, one Avro Avian and a Spartan Three Seater. Despite the ban on flying instruction, training did take place under a Senior Instructor, Archie Reid and one other instructor, but others could be called in from Hanworth if needed. One student was the editor of the *West Herts Post*, R.A. Glenister, who took lessons in a DH60 Moth between September and November 1935 and wrote about the experience in his newspaper. Other participants were staff from the nearby Elstree studios, including Walter Mycroft, the famous film producer for British International Pictures. He presented a cup to the first member of his staff to fly solo. Mycroft had a back disability and had to have the controls of his aeroplane specially modified, but he overcame these difficulties and soon obtained his pilot's licence. He so enjoyed flying that in August 1936 he purchased Spartan Arrow G-AAWZ, which he based at the aerodrome and in which he took film stars for joy rides. Membership of the flying club began to dwindle when most of the film studio staff had gained their licences or moved away, some to Hollywood. The Air Ministry's enforcement of its ban on instruction may also have hastened the decline. The Club eventually closed in late 1937, Maj Shield being dismissed and the two instructors transferring to Hanworth.

Though of poor quality this is the only pre-war photograph taken at Aldenham Aerodrome that has come to light. It was taken just before R.A. Glenister, Editor of the *West Herts Post*, took off for a flying lesson with the Watford branch of the London Air Park Flying Club. Pictured here in front of DH60X Moth G-AAKJ are instructor Archie Reid of Aircraft Exchange & Mart, R.A. Glenister and Major H.S. Shield, Manager of the aerodrome. Glenister took nine or so lessons between September and November 1935 and recounted his experiences in the newspaper. Moth G-AAKJ was withdrawn from use on 7 December 1935. *(Archant Hertfordshire)*

Joyrides were offered at weekends, in a DH60 Moth for 5s (25p), but the more adventurous could try aerobatics in an Avro Avian at 15s (75p). Aircraft Exchange & Mart continued these and their other operations after the demise of the flying club and appointed their ground engineer, T.J. 'Sandy' Sanders as aerodrome manager at the tender age of sixteen! In order to keep the grass surfaces in as good an order as possible Aircraft Exchange & Mart employed three groundsmen, including Joe Warby, the foreman.

Aldenham Aerodrome was not opened officially until 20 April 1935, by which time two hangars and a workshop had been built. The longest landing run was 750 yards, which is slightly more than the length of the licensed runway in 2003 (717 yards). An 'opening' garden party organised by the Aldenham House Club in aid of the British Empire Cancer Campaign took place on 27 July 1935 and included an 'aerial pageant' arranged by Aircraft Exchange & Mart. More than thirty aircraft visited the aerodrome during the afternoon and demonstrations were given by a Cierva C30 Autogiro, Southern Martlet, DH60 Gipsy Moth, Comper Swift, Miles Hawk Major and Monospar ST25. A pony gymkhana took place simultaneously with the air display inside the aerodrome boundary but none of the horses seemed bothered by the constant movements of aircraft above them!

In May 1935 Brian Lewis & Co Ltd, an aircraft broker established in 1930, moved in from Heston and leased one of the hangars from Aircraft Exchange & Mart for their London flying headquarters. The Hon Brian Lewis, who later became Lord Essendon, was a leading racing driver and keen pilot. His company was the distributor for de Havilland aircraft throughout the UK. Its manager was Philip Gordon Marshall and Jock Cameron was the ground engineer. It stayed at the aerodrome until it went into liquidation just before the Second World War.

A regular visitor to Aldenham in the mid-1930s was the Duchess of Bedford, who would park her aeroplane at the aerodrome and travel into London by car. Her log books reveal that she made fourteen flights into Aldenham between June 1935 and July 1936, often accompanied by her personal pilot Flt Lt Rupert C. Preston. The early sorties were flown in DH60G Gipsy Moth G-ABXR but she part-exchanged this for DH60GIII Moth Major G-ACUR in June 1936. Philip Gordon Marshall recalls the occasion when the Duchess flew into Aldenham with Preston to examine 'CUR, which was being offered for sale by Brian Lewis. She did not remove her leather helmet or heavy flying coat throughout the visit, but the helmet was no hindrance as she was very deaf and conversation was inclined to be one-sided! She knew Jock Cameron of old and smiled and nodded amiably as he shouted comments in her ear regarding the finer points of the aeroplane. The 72-year-old

Established in 1930 aircraft brokers Brian Lewis & Company Ltd moved headquarters from Heston Aerodrome to Aldenham in May 1935 and leased a hangar from Aircraft Exchange & Mart Ltd. Brian Lewis was the son of Lord Essendon and also held the licence for Ipswich Aerodrome. This advert appeared in Capt W.E. Johns' *Popular Flying* magazine at the time of the move.

Duchess took off from her airstrip on the Woburn estate on 22 March 1937 to try to complete 200 flying hours and was never seen again.

Aircraft Exchange & Mart was constantly trying to secure a permanent aerodrome licence but the problems with the high tension cables together with a poor surface and little scope for improvement always prevented this. Their proposals soon attracted the attention of the local authorities, both Watford Rural District Council and Aldenham Parish Council voicing their objections to the Air Ministry in November 1935. Two other attempts were made to develop the aerodrome, the first by the Straight Corporation in September 1936. They wanted to establish a 'first-class flying school' and use it generally as an airport as well as a Reserve Training School. The Air Ministry was prepared to accept the possibility of a public-use standard aerodrome being developed but it would be subject to major improvements being undertaken. Handley Page were not keen to have another aerodrome close to their nearby Radlett base but the Air Ministry did not view this as a valid objection. Not surprisingly, no more was heard from the Straight Corporation.

The second attempt, in February 1937, was by Watford Corporation, who were considering developing Aldenham as a standard municipal aerodrome for the town. The Air Ministry was of the opinion that it could be done but would require a good deal of levelling, filling and the diversion or placing underground of the ubiquitous high tension cables. Among the site's other drawbacks were that it was outside the borough, some 4 miles from the town and had difficult rail access. Although the planned extension of the Northern Line to Bushey Heath would have provided a new station near the site, this was abandoned with the outbreak of the Second World War and never revived. Watford Corporation was unhappy that the Air Ministry would not make any financial contribution towards the cost of improvements, conservatively estimated to be £100,000 and again the proposal was not proceeded with, Leavesden eventually becoming the aerodrome for Watford.

A 1936 brochure for the Aldenham House Club includes this statement: 'A nine hole golf course and a polo field are made, and realising the modern trend of transport, a licensed aerodrome with two hangars and three private aeroplanes are at the service of all Members.' The three aeroplanes referred to were not actually registered to the Club but belonged to Aircraft Exchange & Mart. In view of its attachment to the Aldenham House Club, it is surprising that Aldenham was not included in the Automobile Association's 1930s Register of Aircraft Landing Grounds. This listed suitable fields 'conveniently situated close to country hotels, with petrol being readily available from nearby AA approved garages'. Aldenham was, however, included in the third edition of the *Air Pilot* (as Elstree) but not until September 1937 and also in *Jane's All the World's Aircraft* for 1938, again as Elstree.

Aerodrome licences continued to be issued to Aircraft Exchange & Mart on a temporary basis up to the outbreak of the Second World War, the ongoing problems of the poor surface and proximity of the high tension cables precluding any chance of a permanent one. Indeed, the situation got so bad that the licence had to be suspended temporarily in August 1939 as the aerodrome became unserviceable. These problems would not be addressed satisfactorily until well into the forthcoming war. Philip Gordon Marshall, Brian Lewis' manager, made regular flights from Aldenham and his log book entries make interesting references to the state of the grass runways: 'frightening take-off due to rough ground', 'slow take-off due to mud', and 'almost under water, boggy in places'. On one approach to land he had to fly low over the field to clear sheep away from the runway.

The RAF was attracted to the aerodrome and designated it an emergency landing field for the famous RAF Pageants held at nearby Hendon. In 1937 RAF Hendon's Commanding Officer entered into an arrangement with Aircraft Exchange & Mart whereby the three Auxiliary Air Force squadrons based there could use Aldenham as a forced landing ground and for circuit training. The squadrons involved were 600 'City of London', 601 'County of London' and 604 'County of Middlesex', flying Hawker Harts and Demons. This facility was also extended to the communications aircraft (mainly DH82A Tiger Moths) of 24 Squadron. A similar arrangement was made in 1938 with the Commanding Officer of RAF Northolt for 25 Squadron's Gloster Gladiators and later, in 1939, by Spitfire Mk 1s of 65 Squadron. The University of London Air Squadron based at Northolt considered abandoning its forced landing ground at Denham aerodrome in favour of Aldenham but decided not to in view of its poor surface, which it concluded could constitute a danger to trainee pilots.

On 5 January 1938 the Aerial Advertising Company's Avro 504N G-ACZC took off from Aldenham in fog and drizzle towing a banner. Pilot Dick Henderson had planned to fly south to the Tower of London and then along the Thames to Richmond, returning home via Hanworth, Heston and Harrow. Over Richmond the Avro 504N's Lynx engine suffered carburettor icing and stopped. The pilot managed to land safely in Kew Gardens, the Avro finishing up on its nose with only slight damage.
(Via Philip Jarrett)

The aviatrix Beryl Markham stayed at the Aldenham House Club for three months prior to her record-breaking east–west transatlantic crossing in September 1936. During this time she made almost daily visits in an aircraft hired from Brian Lewis to the Percival Aircraft factory at Gravesend, where her Vega Gull *The Messenger* (VP-KCC) was being built. Tom Campbell-Black, who in 1931 had taught Beryl to fly, gave her instruction in full-load take-offs from the Aldenham grass runways. On the day of her epic flight, 4 September, Jim Mollison flew her to RAF Abingdon to begin her journey. The rest is history.

During the summer of 1937 the Hollywood film star Ann Harding was making *Love from a Stranger* at Elstree Studios and her young daughter Jane and a friend were causing havoc on the set. In order to help matters Walter Mycroft enlisted the help of 'Sandy' Sanders in looking after the two girls at the aerodrome, which was only a short walk from where they were staying at the Aldenham House Club. This arrangement lasted for a couple of months, their favourite game being to play pilot and co-pilot in a Bellanca Pacemaker which was up for sale by Brian Lewis in the hangar at the time. One day just before she returned to the USA, Ann Harding arrived at the aerodrome to collect the girls in a brand-new SS Jaguar that she had painted primrose yellow to match her dress! In the autumn of the same year there were only two aircraft resident in Aircraft Exchange & Mart's hangar, the Spartan Arrow belonging to Walter Mycroft and an un-airworthy Bristol Fighter (G-ACAA, ex J8437) owned by A.E. Green & A.P. Fraser.

This Bellanca Pacemaker, built in Delaware in 1931 and pictured at Croydon, visited Aldenham before the war. Hollywood actress Ann Harding's daughter and a friend played in the aircraft while she was filming at Elstree Studios in 1937. The six-seater was powered by a 300hp Wright Whirlwind engine. In July 1941 G-ABNW was impressed into RAF service as DZ209 for use by the Royal Navy and was struck off charge in March 1943. *(The Aeroplane)*

In late 1937 one of Brian Lewis' pilots, Dick Clinton-Holmes, bought a company called Aerial Advertising and based its Avro 504N at the aerodrome for banner towing. This enterprise was short lived, however, as the Avro crashed in Kew Gardens on 5 January 1938 while towing a banner over London.

By 1939 activity at the aerodrome had quietened down and there was talk among Brian Lewis's pilots of an impending war, premonitions which turned out to be correct. In accordance with the Air Navigation Restriction Order which forbade all civil flying without a special permit, Aircraft Exchange & Mart closed the aerodrome at the end of November 1939 and placed a number of old vehicles in strategic positions on the field to prevent enemy aircraft landing. Shortly after this Aircraft Exchange & Mart went into liquidation.

2 'Ubend'um, Wemend'um'

While Aldenham was not an operational station, it nevertheless fulfilled an important but little known role during the Second World War. In August 1940 Fairfield Aviation Ltd, a wholly owned subsidiary of the Redwing Aircraft Company Ltd and a member of the Ministry of Aircraft Production's Civilian Repair Organisation, took over Aldenham for the duration of the war. The company had been set up at Croydon at the outbreak of hostilities to repair Bristol Blenheims, but when that airfield was bombed the firm moved to North Watford where the major part of the Odhams print factory had been requisitioned for them. Fairfield's employed 1,100 people, of whom approximately 200 were based at Aldenham and bussed in daily. While a few skilled operatives transferred from Croydon, the majority, including women, girls and boys had to be recruited and trained, mostly from the Watford area. They proved to be extremely adaptable and within a few weeks became skilled and efficient, working day and night under considerable pressure. Former Fairfield employee Arthur Toms recalls that there were times when he worked all day in the factory at Watford and would then be sent to Aldenham to

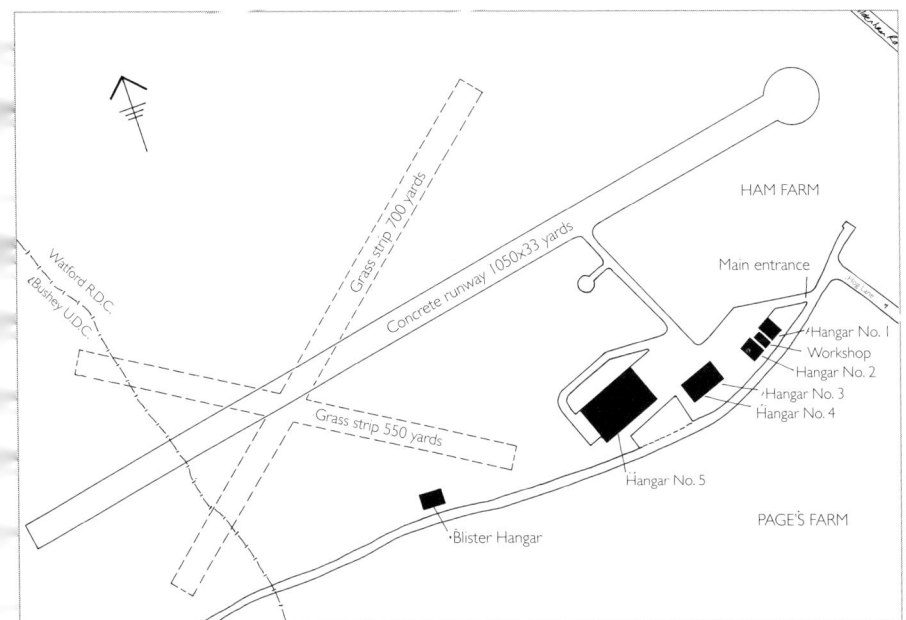

Plan of Aldenham Aerodrome showing the layout of the runways and location of hangars, c. 1944. Page's Farm is at bottom right and Ham Farm at top right. *(GRP)*

work all night. He also remembers long journeys in the blackout between his home in Croydon and Watford/Aldenham, often having to use different routes to avoid bomb damage and after nights spent in air-raid shelters. Fairfield's specialised in Vickers Wellingtons and Westland Lysanders, repairing and/or modifying 473 and 1,217 of them respectively. However, its first job at Aldenham was to remove the old vehicles placed there at the start of the war and to make the aerodrome suitable for test-flying.

Aircraft that had suffered major damage were delivered to the North Watford factory on 'Queen Mary' trailers, often in pieces. When repaired they were towed, minus their wings, to Aldenham Aerodrome, where they were assembled and test-flown. Those that were airworthy and able to cope with the short grass runways were flown in for attention. In 1941 the Blenheims gave way to Miles Masters, then Westland Lysanders which were initially repaired in one of the pre-war hangars while others were worked on in the open under camouflage nets. Geoffrey Davison, a former Fairfield rigger, remembers that this hangar could just accommodate one Lysander and was used by the ladies working in the fabric section. A coke-burning stove was the sole source of heat and they were all blissfully unaware of the

explosive nature of the dope-laden air as they sat around it eating their lunch! On another occasion, 16-year-old Geoffrey climbed into the cockpit of a Lysander and while pretending to fly it pressed the gun-firing button. Contrary to strict orders, the aircraft had been delivered armed and Geoffrey got the fright of his life when both guns in the wheel spats fired a round! Luckily for him, no one witnessed or heard what he had done!

Facilities at Aldenham improved considerably in 1942 when the Ministry of Aircraft Production constructed three new hangars, an 'R' type and two Super Robins. They also laid a 1,050yd concrete runway, enabling Wellingtons to be flown in for repair/modification. The first three to arrive were flown in by RAF pilots in April 1943. Because the runway had been camouflaged by a surface dressing of tar and green wood chippings which made it extremely slippery, two of the Wellingtons overshot. As a result of this incident all Wellingtons were delivered and test-flown by Ministry of Aircraft Production test pilot Flt Lt Tim 'Timber' Woods, RAFVR. It is probable that the Wellingtons were first flown into nearby Radlett aerodrome for onward delivery to Aldenham by 'Timber' Woods, but it has not been possible to obtain confirmation of this. Woods commuted

As a repaired Vickers Wellington fuselage arrives at Elstree the towing crew pose by their Ministry of Aircraft Production lorry before driving the few yards to the main assembly hangar. Escorted by police motorcycle riders it had been towed the 5 miles from Fairfield Aviation's repair factory at St Albans Road, Watford. The pre-war flying control structure can be seen attached to the right of the left-hand hangar. *(Redwing Ltd, via J. Lane)*

The partly-covered fuselage of a Vickers Wellington pictured at Fairfield Aviation's Watford factory. Once the fuselage was completed it was mounted on a two-wheel trolley and towed by road to Elstree for final assembly and flight-testing. *(Redwing Ltd, via J. Lane)*

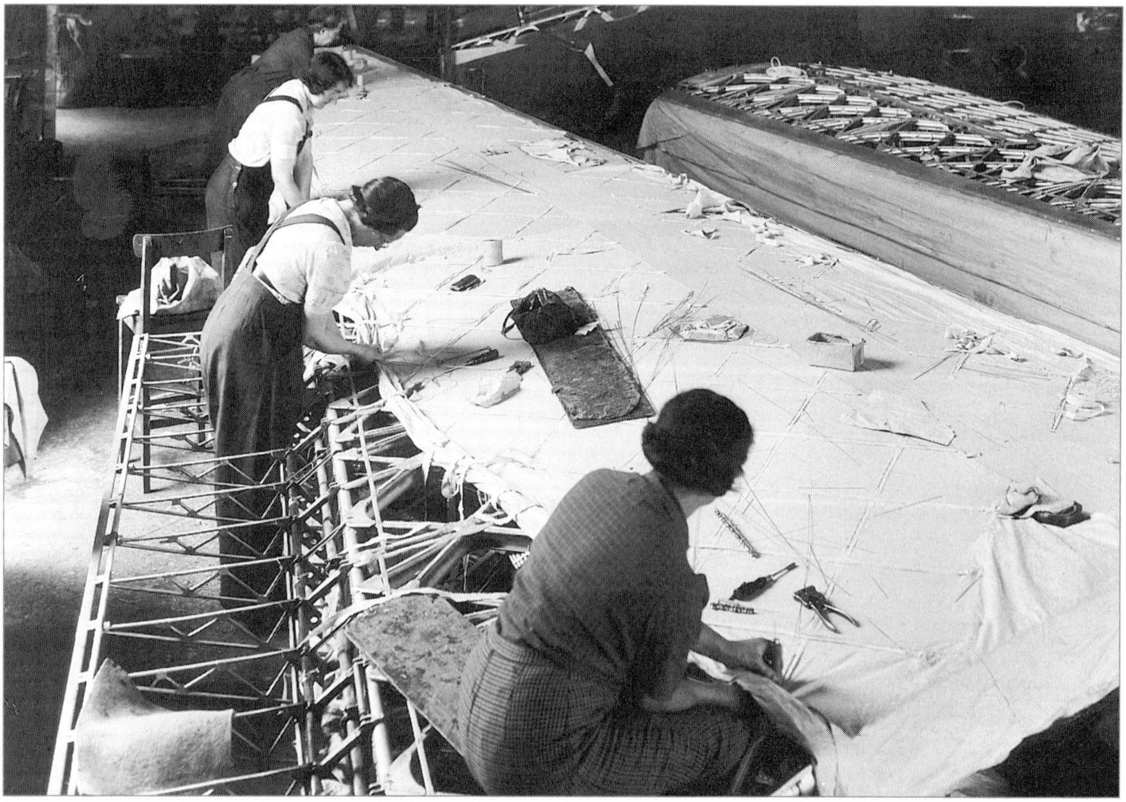

Women employees of Fairfield Aviation's Watford plant are covering Wellington main planes with Irish linen. The ingenious basket-weave geodetic structure with its high strength/weight ratio pioneered by Barnes Wallis is clearly visible. *(Redwing Ltd, via J. Lane)*

Reconditioned Bristol Pegasus radial engines ready for installing into Vickers Wellingtons. The chalk number on the cowling of the engine nearest the camera denoted the airframe to which the Pegasus would be fitted. *(Redwing Ltd, via J. Lane)*

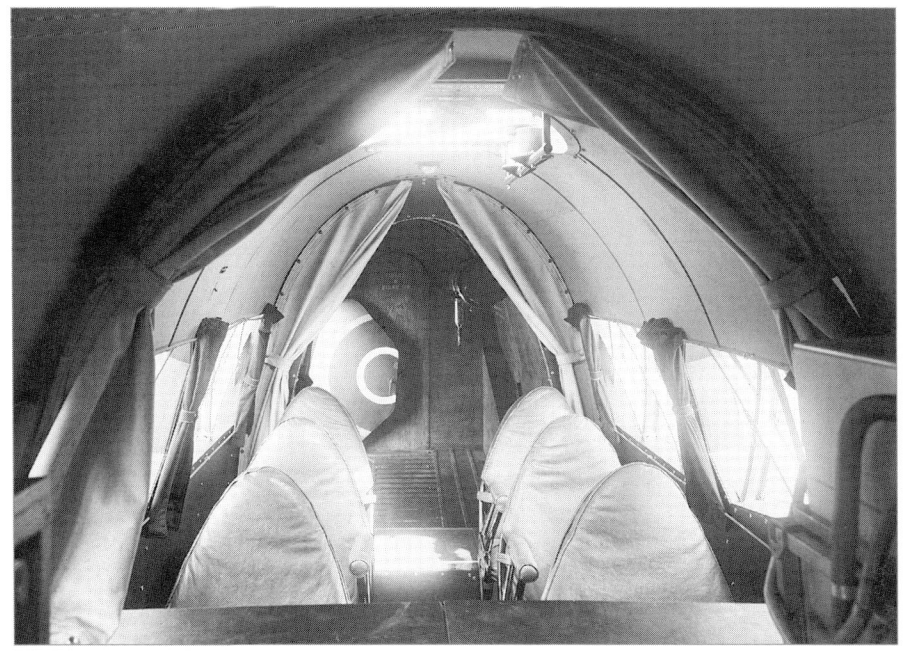

Looking aft in the passenger cabin of a Wellington after conversion by Fairfield Aviation. In response to an urgent requirement for a transport aircraft for use in the Middle East hundreds of Wellington bombers were converted for troop carrying. All military equipment was removed and very basic seating installed. *(Redwing Ltd, via J. Lane)*

Fairfield Aviation's main assembly hangar at Elstree Aerodrome filled with Vickers Wellingtons in various stages of construction. Half the aircraft are standard bombers, while those nearest the camera have been converted into freight/transport Mk XVIs, with noses and tails stripped of armament and turrets faired over. This photograph was taken at the entrance to the main hangar, looking west. *(Redwing Ltd, via J. Lane)*

to the aerodrome from White Waltham in a variety of aircraft including Spitfires, Hurricanes, a Tipsy Trainer and the company's hack, Monospar ST25 G-AGDN. Repaired or modified Lysanders were often flown out and delivered to RAF Maintenance Units by women pilots of the Air Transport Auxiliary (ATA) attached to No. 5 Ferry Pilots Pool, based at nearby Hatfield. Lettice Curtis, the well-known ATA pilot, made eleven of these deliveries between April 1941 and March 1942. John Ausden, then a schoolboy, recalls cycling to the aerodrome one summer evening around this time and seeing approximately ten Lysanders in front of the hangars. While he was there a Spitfire landed, the pilot transferred to one of the Lysanders and flew off, returning 20–30 minutes later to take off again in the Spitfire. This was presumably 'Timber' Woods carrying out one of his many test flights.

Built as a standard Vickers Wellington Mk 1C, DV761 is seen in the Fairfield main hangar at Elstree during modification to Mk XVI configuration. Though the nose and tail turrets have been removed and the positions faired over they have yet to be covered with fabric. This Wellington served with No. 415 Squadron before being struck off RAF charge in April 1946. *(Redwing Ltd, via J. Lane)*

Under a shroud of secrecy, at least fourteen Lysanders were converted for use by the Special Operations Executive (SOE) for ferrying secret agents to and from occupied Europe. The modifications included installing an up-rated Bristol Mercury engine, fitting a 150-gallon long-range tank under the fuselage, addition of an enlarged oil tank, and a ladder to facilitate easier access. The removal of armament, armour and other items to reduce weight provided accommodation for three passengers. Fairfield's also converted a number of Lysander Mk3As to target tugs. To assist with the large number of Pegasus, Hercules and Mercury engines installed in the Wellingtons and Lysanders, the Bristol Engine Company's representative, Ted Williams, was permanently on site.

Fairfield's repaired, modified or refitted a total of 1,809 aircraft, which in addition to the 473 Wellingtons and 1,217 Lysanders, consisted of 67 Miles Masters and

A Vickers Wellington Mk XVI freighter, recently converted by Fairfield Aviation, sits in the sun at the eastern end of Elstree's newly laid runway prior to being ferried to its next unit. *(Redwing Ltd, via J. Lane)*

52 others, including Bristol Blenheims and various Hawker biplanes – Harts, Hectors, Hinds and Audax. Of the total, 693 were repaired in situ all over the country by mobile gangs sent out from Watford, the motto on the back of their jerseys reading 'Ubend'um, Wemend'um'. The demand from Bomber Command was so great that between July 1941 and April 1943 a temporary branch of the company was set up at RAF Hemswell in Lincolnshire specifically to repair Wellingtons. When this deployment ended, Aldenham concentrated solely on the Wellington. The last aircraft repaired by the company was a Wellington Mk XV11 for Coastal Command; after it was flown out of Aldenham, on 10 October 1945, Fairfield Aviation and the aerodrome closed down. The Ministry of Labour found nearly all Fairfield's displaced workers jobs in other local industries. During its time

Fairfield engineers working on a Wellington's Bristol Pegasus radial engine in the entrance of the main hangar at Elstree. Each component of the aircraft bears the chalked number '360'. *(Redwing Ltd, via J. Lane)*

This sequence of three photographs was taken at Elstree on 10 October 1945 on the occasion of the departure of the last of 473 Vickers Wellingtons repaired or modified by Fairfield Aviation Ltd. Powered by two Bristol Hercules XVI series radial engines, this Coastal Command Wellington features nose radar installed for training radar operators for the Wellington G.R. Mk XVIII. *(West Herts Post)*

in Hertfordshire, it was not all work and no play for Fairfield's workers. The daily grind was relieved with concerts and social gatherings in aid of local prisoners of war and the Red Cross. The workers presented shows at local camps and hospitals and were once selected for a 'Works Wonders' BBC broadcast. They organised a weekly 6d (2½p) collection among themselves and as a result were able to donate £18 each week to Church Farm Hospital, Aldenham, thus earning the distinction of being the first factory in Britain to adopt a Red Cross hospital.

By August 1943 No. 124 ATC Gliding School had been formed at Aldenham under Flt Lt Jim Ford, a pre-war charter pilot based at Croydon. The school used mostly Slingsby Cadets, but also had use of a Slingsby Tutor, Slingsby Two Seater, Grunau Sailplane and a Dagling. They were usually launched by balloon winch but with the occasional aero tow. About sixteen ATC cadets were accepted for each course of eight weekends' duration. They spent two hours each weekend in the classroom at the rear of their blister hangar learning theory of flight, elementary

Slingsby T.7 Cadet TX.1 RA991 built by Enham Industries, landing at Elstree with Flt Lt Denis Evans at the controls, 28 April 1946. The presence in the background of three Vickers Wellingtons is curious as the last one was supposed to have left Fairfield Aviation in October 1945. An RAF Airspeed Oxford is parked beside the main hangar. (West Herts Post, via Denis M. Evans)

Officers and instructors of No. 124 ATC Gliding School with a Slingsby T.7 Cadet at an open day and passing out parade at Aldenham in April 1946. No. 124 was one of 78 Gliding Schools across the country. (West Herts Post, via Denis M. Evans)

Flying Officer Harry Davies, Flt Lt Jim Ford, Group Captain Smith AFC and Squadron Leader Marsh? with cadet Willis at a passing-out ceremony at Aldenham in April 1946. The buildings at the side of the hangar still exist; that on the left subsequently became the Elstree Flying Club clubhouse. *(West Herts Post, via Denis M. Evans)*

Group Captain Smith AFC with Flt Lt Jim R. Ford and cadets of No. 124 ATC Gliding School chatting around a Slingsby T.7 Cadet at Elstree in April 1946. *(West Herts Post, via Denis M. Evans)*

Cierva C.30A DR624 pictured at Elstree, on 6 April 1945. Licence-built by A.V. Roe Ltd at Manchester this Autogiro began life as G-ACWF in July 1934. The Autogiro remained with the Cierva Autogiro Company Ltd at Hanworth, most of the time in storage, until impressed into RAF service in mid-1941 as DR624. Initially DR624 flew with the Autogiro Section of 74 Wing Calibration Flight at RAF Duxford. Following a landing accident at Duxford in February 1942 DR624 was repaired and assigned to No. 1448 Radar Calibration Flight, also at Duxford. When this unit was disbanded in June 1943 and merged with 75 Wing Calibration Flight to become 529 Squadron, DR624 moved to RAF Halton and was given the code letters KX-L. It remained with the squadron until delivered to No. 5 M.U. at RAF Kemble in November 1945 and put in storage. In April 1946 DR624 was sold to Fairey Aviation Company Ltd and re-registered G-AHMI the following month. The company purchased two other C.30s with the intention of using them to give Fairey pilots rotary wing experience during the building of the Fairey Gyrodyne. G-AHMI was dismantled in July 1947 after its Certificate of Airworthiness expired and was given to the Shuttleworth Trust at Old Warden where it languished for many years. During the 1990s the Autogiro was restored to non-flying condition and repainted as DR624 and coded KX-L once more. It is currently exhibited at Duxford.

These photographs of DR624, coded KX-L, were taken during a visit to Elstree, from Lacey Green. Vickers Wellingtons modified by Fairfield Aviation and awaiting ferrying to transport units can be seen in the background. *(RTR Collection)*

This view of Cierva C.30A DR624 at Elstree is of particular interest because it is the only known photograph showing the Allied Expeditionary Air Force Communication Squadron presence at Elstree. Just visible beneath the starboard wing of the Wellington at left can be seen what appears to be an Auster outside the Squadron's blister hangar.
(RTR Collection)

aerodynamics, glider handling and meteorology. Each cadet had about fifty glider flights. Flt Lt Denis Evans, the Chief Flying Instructor, would sometimes fly over from Woodley near Reading in his Miles Hawk Major (G-ADMW) and give the top-scoring cadet a 30-minute air experience flight in this aircraft, or in a locally based DH Tiger Moth or Auster. Due to increased powered flying activity at Elstree the school moved to Hendon in October 1947.

A detachment of the Allied Expeditionary Air Force (AEAF) Communication Squadron arrived in August 1944, occupying a blister hangar and a couple of wooden huts. Three Austers and a DH94 Moth Minor were attached to the squadron but other visiting flights were operated by Avro Ansons and Percival Proctors. The AEAF became the Supreme HQ Allied Expeditionary Force (SHAEF) on 15 October 1944 and was disbanded in July 1945. During its short stay at Aldenham more than 70 movements were recorded, Air Vice-Marshal Sir Philip Wigglesworth, Dep. Chief of Staff (Air) SHAEF and later Dep. Air C-in-C, Germany, being a regular passenger. On one famous occasion General Wavell arrived by mistake at Aldenham, in a Lockheed Hudson, while his reception party was waiting patiently for him at Hendon!

Despite its important role, the aerodrome received minimal attention from the enemy during the war. Only one bomb fell, a high explosive one, outside the pre-war hangars on 6 January 1941. It penetrated fifteen feet into the soft clay before exploding and compressing the clay, forming a large cavern. Fortunately there were no casualties and little damage was caused. Guard dogs belonging to the RAF Regiment were used for security purposes and the aerodrome was patrolled at night from May 1942 to October 1944 by a small detachment of the Home Guard from the Middlesex Regiment.

CIVIL AIRPORTS—No. 1

Light Plane photo

ELSTREE AIRPORT, Hertfordshire

Civil Airport controlled by London Aero & Motor Services, Ltd.
No Customs facilities available.

Airport Manager: G. F. P. O'Farrell.
Chief Engineer: E. Chick.
Position: 0° 19′ 30″ W. 51° 39′ 15″ N.
Field Elevation: 300 ft. A.M.S.L.
Obstructions: High tension cables 400 yards to North of airfield.
Airfield Lighting: Nil.
Telephone No.: ELStree 1677.
Transport Facilities: Nearest bus service, one mile. 141 bus from Edgware Tube Station to Elstree village. 306 bus from Watford to By-pass or village.
Airfield Information: One concrete runway. Q.D.M. 270°—90°. 1,115 yards long by 100 feet wide. One grass run, S.W.—N.E., 900 yards. Tarmac taxi-track and parking area.

Hangars: Three, used by civil and club aircraft. Hangarage facilities available to all aircraft.
Servicing: Major facilities available.
Refuelling: Two pumps. 73 and 87 octane.
Refreshments: Light refreshments only at present. Licensed bar.
Hotels: Edgwarebury Country Club, Elstree. Aldenham Lodge Hotel, Radlett.
Distance to London: 12 miles.
Radio Facilities: Nil.
Flying Club: United Services Flying Club. Fleet consists of three Austers and one Proctor. Tuition to "B" licence standard. "Hire-fly-yourself" service available.
Charter: Light charter aircraft available at B.A.C.A. standard rates.

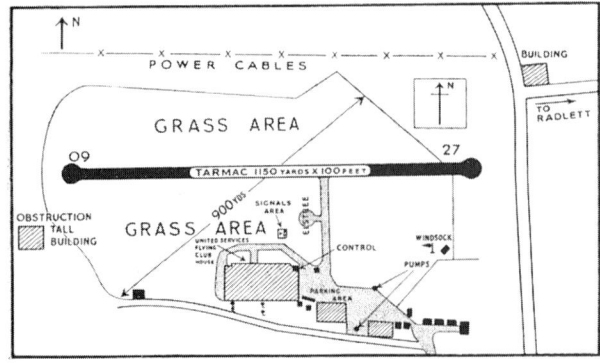

N.B.—This page is the first of a series which, used in conjunction with the *Light Plane* British Airport Map, will prove a valuable help to the private flier. Reprints of this page are available upon application to the Editor.

Next month: White Waltham.

This information on Elstree Aerodrome was published in the February 1948 issue of *The Light Plane and Private Owner*. *(RTR Collection)*

3 Postwar Heavyweights and Lightweights

With the lifting of restrictions on powered flying after the war, the aerodrome re-opened and soon attracted numerous flying clubs, private owners, air-taxi and charter companies, making it one of the most popular in the London area. It was managed as 'The London Flying Centre' by Grosvenor Square Garages, a West End car-hire group, which based a fleet of light aircraft at the aerodrome from January 1946. It traded as London Aero & Motor Services (LAMS) and also hired aircraft to the United Services Flying Club (USFC), as well as offering hangarage, maintenance, aerial photography and aero-towing for sailplanes. The aerodrome manager was Wg Cdr Royce Wilkinson. It held an 'Airfield House Warming' on 9 June 1946 which included a small air display and competitions. The company used three Auster Autocrats and one Percival Proctor, which were operated in close association with its car-hire organisation. A Daimler car would collect the

This excellent view of Elstree Aerodrome, looking west, was taken on 27 July 1947. Despite its appearance the runway had been laid only five years earlier. In order to accommodate Vickers Wellingtons the runway was extended beyond the eastern boundary – the gap in the hedge of the field in the foreground bears witness to this. Five years later the Hilfield Reservoir would dominate the area to the left of the lane that passes to the left of the main hangar. *(Aerofilms)*

passenger from their home or office and drive them to the aerodrome, where one of LAMS' Austers would fly them to the nearest airfield to their destination. On arrival here another courtesy car was waiting to complete the passenger's journey. The rates for this operation were from 1s 6d (7½p) a mile for a minimum journey of 100 miles. The USFC catered mainly for service and ex-service personnel of the civil and military services and boasted that it was the nearest flying club to London's West End. It organised an 'Air Display & International Rally' on 27 July 1947. In addition to Austers and Proctors, it operated DH82A Tiger Moths and a Taylorcraft Plus D, as well as a Link Trainer. Also, a wide variety of ad hoc charters were undertaken by LAMS under the watchful eye of its Managing Director, Dr Graham Humby.

"I'm an 'A' PILOT"

London's most successful and nearest Flying Centre —only 12 miles from Baker Street—can give comprehensive training for the Private Pilot's "A" Licence, and full Flying and Ground Courses for the Commercial Pilot's "B" Licence.

Instructor's Endorsement Courses also available.

Apply to Secretary for full particulars.

Thanks to
UNITED SERVICES FLYING CLUB
ELSTREE AERODROME . MIDDX.
Telephone: ELSTREE 1677

Air-to-air view of C. Nepean Bishop, chief flying instructor of the United Services Flying Club (USFC) operated by London Aero Motor Services (LAMS), flying cream Auster Autocrat G-AGXJ over the LMS railway line a mile to the east of Elstree Aerodrome on 26 May 1946. Originally purchased new in 1946 by Grosvenor Square Garages G-AGXJ was part of a fleet of three Austers and a Percival Proctor operated from Elstree on charter and instruction work. Flying rates in January 1947 were £3 15s per hour. In 1953 G-AGXJ was sold in France and became F-BGRX. *(EJR)*

Postwar Heavyweights and Lightweights

Auster J.1 Autocrat G-AHCL joined the fleet of LAMS in June 1946 and is seen here over Elstree on 20 April 1949 after it was sold to a private owner. The photograph is interesting because it features the blister hangar, seen below the Auster's starboard wheel, and the early postwar home of John 'Tubby' Simpson whose company Simpson's Aeroservices was based at Elstree for more than twenty years. For a short period during the war the blister hangar was the home of an Allied Expeditionary Air Force Communication Squadron. After the war it was used by No. 124 ATC Gliding School and by the Ultra Light Aircraft Association (ULAA) from October 1947. The area to the left of the track running diagonally from right to left is now covered by the Hilfield Reservoir. Auster G-AHCL was still extant in 2003. *(EJR)*

This aerial photograph of Elstree Aerodrome was taken during the air display held on 27 July 1947. All six hangars, including the blister, are clearly visible, the largest being No. 5, the Type 'R' hangar, built during the war to house the Fairfield Aviation operation. Just about visible is the name ELSTREE, painted in 10ft high letters next to the signals area near the taxiway/runway intersection. The air display attracted 12,000 visitors and additional car parking had to be provided in the adjoining fields seen at the top of the photograph. *(Aerofilms)*

In the spring of 1946, Dr Humby decided that freight would be a more profitable operation and to this end he acquired a fleet of almost new Halifax C. Mk8s direct from Handley Page. He consulted a wartime heavy bomber pilot on the feasibility of operating Halifaxes from Elstree so as to employ the company's engineers already based there. The pilot's assessment was that with at least a 15 knot wind on the westerly (uphill) runway and using an approach speed just above the stall, it would be possible, providing weight was at a minimum. In the event the first ferry flight from nearby Radlett made a heavy landing but was otherwise successful. Five more followed in July/August 1946 and conversion to freighters began. They emerged resplendent in a royal blue livery with white lettering and bearing the names of prominent seaports. G-AHZN was the first to receive its Certificate of Airworthiness, on 28 August and the others followed at monthly intervals. Unfortunately the early days of the freight operation were marred by two incidents. The port undercarriage of G-AHZM collapsed at Elstree during a Certificate of Airworthiness test flight on 16 September and the aircraft was cannibalised for spares, languishing behind the main hangar until January 1950. Then, on the 26th of that month, G-AHZN *Port of London* was lost off Le Zoute on the Belgian coast when it ditched while on a flight from Bergamo to Heathrow with a cargo of fruit. Things then settled down and for the rest of 1946 the remaining four Halifaxes plied continuously to destinations throughout Europe, Africa and the Middle East, carrying cargoes which included fruit, ships' spares and oil drilling machinery. However, Elstree served only as a maintenance base for the Halifaxes, the empty aircraft being positioned at Heathrow for their onward flights.

By December 1946 it had become apparent to LAMS that Elstree was too small to operate its Halifax fleet, particularly in view of its short runway and the earlier crash landing incident. Therefore, on 14 December, it started to move its freight operation to a new base at Stansted, but retained the passenger side of the business at Elstree. This was in the charge of its manager Mr A.J.I. Temple-West and employed

Handley Page Halifax H.P. 70 C. Mk 8 G-AHZO *Port of London* at Elstree in 1946. In March 1949 this freighter passed to Skyflight Ltd only to be dismantled at Stansted three months later. In the space of two years LAMS acquired 26 Halifaxes but only half this number actually entered service. *(EJR)*

LAMS' Handley Page H.P. 70 C. Mk 8 Halifax G-AIWK *Port of Sydney* photographed during a low pass over Elstree on 27 July 1947. The turquoise blue freighter, which was en route from Stansted to Milan with a full load, made several low passes before heading on its journey to Italy. G-AIWK had recently returned from a 27,000-mile round-the-world flight that ended at Stansted on 5 June, arriving with a cargo of seven tons of dripping, a gift from the people of Australia. The arrival at Stansted marked the official opening of the airport for civil freight aircraft. G-AIWK returned to Sydney but in December 1947 it was scrapped at Mascot in Sydney, Australia after being vandalised. *(EJR)*

LAMS' Handley Page H.P. 70 C. Mk 8 Halifax G-AHZM after its first civil test flight when the port undercarriage leg collapsed. Rather than repair the damage the aircraft was towed to an area behind the main hangar where it languished outside for many years (see page 155) gradually being stripped of its vital parts to keep the rest of the LAMS fleet flying. In January 1950 the scrapmen arrived and removed what was left of what had become a familiar Elstree landmark. *(EJR)*

Handley Page H.P. 70 C. Mk 8 Halifax G-AHZL *Port of Oslo* beating up Elstree Aerodrome on Sunday, July 27, 1947 at the start of the Air Display and International Rally organised by London Aero & Motor Services (LAMS). While the Halifax made several low passes the display commentator, LAMS' managing director Dr Graham Humby, commented upon the aircraft's lousiness! After LAMS was wound up in July 1948 G-AHZL languished a while at Stansted before being dismantled in June the following year. *(EJR)*

Postwar Heavyweights and Lightweights

twenty staff. The passenger fleet had increased to four Auster Autocrats, two Percival Proctors and four Airspeed Consuls, but not all of these were registered to LAMS, some being leased from another Elstree-based charter company, probably Atlas Aviation. By the end of 1947 cargo work had diminished and at the same time a subsidiary freight venture in Australia also failed. The company found less and less work and to add to their problems their Managing Director, Dr Humby, was seriously ill in hospital. Without his drive, efforts to secure new work failed and sadly LAMS' operations from Stansted ceased by June 1948. The Elstree passenger business followed suit in 1950. Had the company survived only a little longer it would undoubtedly have been fully employed on the Berlin Airlift.

Immediately after the war, one of the pre-war hangars was used as a test laboratory by Monaco Motor & Engineering Co. Ltd. This company was based in Kings Langley and had designed a neat flat-four aero engine suitable for light aircraft. At least one engine was designed and tested but was never fitted to an aircraft. The company soon disappeared without trace.

Below: This view of Elstree looking north east, taken during the air display held on 27 July 1947, features the short-lived blister hangar at left and the cannibalised remains of the LAMS Handley Page Halifax G-AHZM behind Hangar No 5. Most of the foreground area this side of the lane now forms the eastern edge of Hilfield Reservoir. *(Aerofilms)*

LAMS Halifax G-AHZN pictured in the sea off Knocke, Belgium after it was ditched during a flight from Milan to Heathrow early on the morning of 26 September 1946. Carrying a cargo of grapes the Halifax was captained by Sqn Ldr G. Coleman, who got into difficulties in the darkness over the North Sea. Unable to receive any radio directional bearings the pilot elected to ditch off the coast but hit a submerged breakwater. The crew of three managed to swim ashore but a Norwegian passenger was trapped in the aircraft and drowned. *(RTR Collection)*

LAMS Handley Page H.P. 70 C. Mk 8 Halifax G-AHZN, formerly PP244 with the RAF, pictured at Elstree in August 1946 shortly after it received its first Certificate of Airworthiness, the first of the LAMS Halifax fleet to be certificated. A few days later this Halifax was lost after ditching off Knocke, Belgium – see page 49. *(EJR)*

LAMS Handley Page H.P. 70 C. Mk 8 Halifax G-AHZO *Port of London* parked by the taxiway at Elstree Aerodrome in 1946. Originally assembled at nearby Radlett aerodrome this and five other RAF C. Mk 8 Halifaxes were acquired by Dr Graham Humby, ferried to Elstree and converted for freight work. Elstree remained LAMS' maintenance base until the entire operation moved to Stansted in December 1946. G-AHZO was sold to Skyflight Ltd in 1949 and was dismantled at Stansted shortly after. *(EJR)*

LAMS Halifax G-AHZK, pictured at Elstree in 1947, was named *Port of Naples*. In March 1949 the freighter was sold to Skyflight Ltd at Stansted, where it was broken up a few months later. After Dr Graham Humby was taken seriously ill with tuberculosis he had to step down as MD. The company subsequently fell into difficulty and in July 1948 LAMS went out of business. Had it survived a few weeks longer the company would no doubt have found ample work on the Berlin Airlift. *(RTR)*

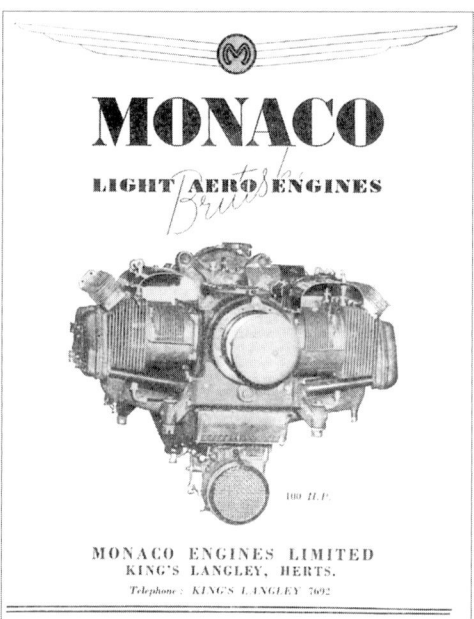

This advertisement for Monaco Engines Ltd appeared in the September 1948 issue of *The Lightplane and Private Owner*. (RTR Collection)

Below: This low-level aerial photograph of the entrance to Elstree Aerodrome taken in July 1947 features the two original pre-war hangars and workshop. Aircraft Exchange & Mart occupied No. 1 nearest the camera and during the war Fairfield Aviation used it for storing aircraft components. After the war Monaco Engines Ltd moved in but had disappeared by 1949. By January 1950 the front had been bricked-up and 7ft-wide doors installed, which precluded further use as a hangar and thereafter it reverted to storage. Brian Lewis & Company Ltd leased hangar No.2 from Aircraft Exchange & Mart from 1935 and during the early part of the war Fairfield Aviation used it for repairing Westland Lysanders. It was subsequently used for storage purposes. Both hangars suffered considerable storm damage in the 1960s and had collapsed completely by 1969. The workshop in between the two hangars was used jointly by Aircraft Exchange & Mart and Brian Lewis before the war and as an engine store by Fairfield Aviation for the duration. It suffered a similar fate to the hangars but was rebuilt and is currently used by a vehicle maintenance company. (Aerofilms)

The next company to commence charter operations at Elstree was Atlas Aviation, which moved in from Heston in October 1946 but it was short-lived, closing down less than a year later. During its short life it operated three Percival Proctors, four Airspeed Consuls and a Miles Gemini.

Airborne Taxi Services started ad hoc short-range charter operations from Elstree in December 1946. Its fleet of light single-engine aircraft consisted of a Piper Cub, Auster 5, Taylorcraft Plus D and DH87B Hornet Moth during its six-year life. It was engaged on a series of Army cooperation flights during 1949/50 and pleasure flights at airshows in the summer. It stopped flying in late 1952, at which time it was operating only the Hornet Moth and Taylorcraft.

Another early postwar air taxi/charter company was Dennis Aviation, which set up a subsidiary base at Elstree in 1947. With three Percival Proctors, two Airspeed

Airspeed A.S. 65 Consul G-AHMA, was sold new to Elstree-based Atlas Aviation Ltd in 1946 and is pictured at Elstree shortly after its arrival. It was written off at Lyon en route from Gatwick to Geneva on 24 December. Formed at Heston in October 1946 Atlas transferred operations to Elstree soon after. Operating a fleet of three Proctors, four Consuls and a Miles Gemini, Atlas ceased trading in late 1947. *(EJR)*

Atlas Aviation Ltd operated a subsidiary company named Guernsey Air Charter, also based at Elstree and Airspeed A.S. 65 Consul G-AIDW was used on flights to the Channel Islands during 1947. After the company ceased operations the Consul was sold to Dexford Motors at Southend and was finally scrapped there in late 1951. *(EJR)*

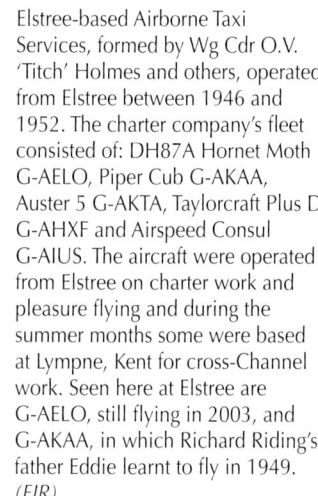

Elstree-based Airborne Taxi Services, formed by Wg Cdr O.V. 'Titch' Holmes and others, operated from Elstree between 1946 and 1952. The charter company's fleet consisted of: DH87A Hornet Moth G-AELO, Piper Cub G-AKAA, Auster 5 G-AKTA, Taylorcraft Plus D G-AHXF and Airspeed Consul G-AIUS. The aircraft were operated from Elstree on charter work and pleasure flying and during the summer months some were based at Lympne, Kent for cross-Channel work. Seen here at Elstree are G-AELO, still flying in 2003, and G-AKAA, in which Richard Riding's father Eddie learnt to fly in 1949. *(EJR)*

Dennis Aviation Ltd, first established at Croydon in 1946 equipped with Percival Proctors, Avro Anson 1s and a couple of Airspeed Consuls, set up another base at Elstree the following year. By 1950 the company's operations had been absorbed by Transair, which in turn went into liquidation in 1951. Pictured at Elstree in 1947 is Dennis Aviation's Percival Proctor 5 G-AHTL, sold in France as F-OAOZ in 1954. *(EJR)*

Consuls and four Avro Ansons, it had started operations at Croydon in August 1946 and undertook charters to many parts of Europe. Its operations were gradually integrated with those of Transair until in September 1951 the transfer was completed and the company moved out of Elstree.

In May 1947 yet another small charter company was formed at Elstree in the shape of Pullman Airways. It flew passenger charters to Europe and North Africa with a single Airspeed Consul until 27 February 1948 when this aircraft unfortunately crashed into the Mediterranean with the loss of all those on board. The company then ceased operations after less than a year.

The last of the early postwar charter companies to operate from Elstree was Trans-World Charter Ltd. It began long-distance passenger and freight services in May 1948 with two Vickers Vikings and shared its base with Bovingdon. Its major business was the transporting of ship's crews all over Europe, North Africa and the Middle East, together with freight, which mainly consisted of ship's spares, fruit and vegetables. In late 1948 the company was involved in the Berlin Airlift, albeit in a relatively minor role, the two Vikings recording 118 sorties in a seven-week period ending on 14 November. Trans-World Charter set up its own maintenance

base at Bovingdon in July 1950, which coincided with the purchase of its third Viking, but within a year it had moved to Elstree. It ceased trading on 3 December 1951 when it was sold to Southend-based Crewsair and all operations continued under this title until the company was wound up in February 1953. While it would appear from the fleets of the six foregoing charter companies that the aerodrome was awash with a large number of aircraft, there were actually never more than about twelve based there at any one time. This was because some were only kept for short periods, were sold or leased to other resident operators or were written-off in accidents. (This figure does not include the six LAMS Halifaxes, which were only resident from July to December 1946.)

In October 1946 the Ultra Light Aircraft Association (ULAA) came into being and its Experimental Group occupied the blister hangar after the ATC Gliding School vacated it in October 1947. Arthur W.J.G. Ord-Hume was a leading member of the Group. It worked on Taylor Watkinson Ding-Bat G-AFJA, Benes-Mraz Bibi G-AGSR and Zaunkoenig G-ALUA.

The creation of a new reservoir immediately south of the aerodrome necessitated the demolition of the blister hangar, which meant that the ULAA had to re-locate. As a consequence it moved to Redhill in January 1950 and eventually became the Popular Flying Association. In the 1940/50s the American Embassy Flying Club, Elliotts (later Marconi Elliotts Flying Club for their employees at Borehamwood), Handley Page Flying Club, set up by David Ogilvy in 1953, and Bristol Aeroplane Company's London Office Flying Club were resident at the aerodrome. After the departure of the ATC Gliding School in October 1947, another gliding club was formed in July of the following year. Known as the Aerotec Group, it operated BAC Drone G-ADSB, configured as a two-seat glider by removing its engine and a converted 'Beaverette' armoured car was used for towing. However, Arthur W.J.G. Ord-Hume remembers that nobody ever managed a circuit and the flights were restricted to straight launches up and down the runway, or next to it on the grass. The Group shared the blister hangar with the ULAA and was disbanded when its home was demolished in January 1950.

Trans-World Charter Vickers Type 498 Viking 1A G-AHOT taking off from Elstree in January 1951. First registered in September 1946 and operated by British European Airways, G-AHOT was acquired by Trans-World Charter Ltd in January 1948 and remained with the company until it ceased trading in December 1951. Following a period with Crewsair this Viking was sold abroad as ZS-DKH in October 1954. *(Aerofilms)*

Three photographs of the Heath Parasol G-AFZE taken in the vicinity of the ULAA's blister hangar at Elstree. Robert Parker began building his American-designed Heath Parasol G-AFZE in 1936 but it was not completed until after the war when it was taken to Elstree and took up residence in the ULAA blister hangar. Powered by a 24hp Blackburne Tomtit inverted V-twin engine the Parasol made its first flight, but only just, in September 1948. Its first proper flight took place at Elstree in January 1949 when the top photograph was taken. The Parasol was cancelled from the British civil register in June 1996. *(EJR and Arthur W.J.G. Ord-Hume)*

The silver Comper Swift G-ABUS photographed outside the ULAA blister hangar on its first arrival at Elstree on Sunday 22 August 1948. Owned by A.J. Linnell, but on long-term loan to Tony Cole, this Swift was later doped overall black and named *Black Magic*. During the 1940s and 1950s Cole and David Ogilvy successfully raced it. *(Arthur W.J.G. Ord-Hume)*

Austen Chamberlain's blue and silver *Oscar* glider was another occupant of Elstree's blister hangar and is pictured in June 1949. Operated by the short-lived Aerotec Group *Oscar* rarely became airborne. It began life in 1935 as the B.A.C. Drone G-ADSB but was converted into B.A.C. VII glider configuration by the London Gliding Club in 1938. *(Arthur W.J.G. Ord-Hume)*

The Brunswick Zaunkoenig G-ALUA, belonging to ULAA founder Ron Clegg, lived in the blister hangar at Elstree during 1949/50. Powered by a 51hp Zundapp engine it was designed by students at Brunswick Technical High School in Germany and was first flown in 1945. In recent years the Zaunkoenig was returned to Germany and registered D-EBCQ. It is currently on static display at the Deutsches Museum. *(Arthur W.J.G. Ord-Hume)*

Two unused Airspeed Horsa troop-carrying gliders arrived by road from Radlett in 1948 and were stored, dismantled, on wasteland behind the main hangar. One was purchased for £5 by Arthur W.J.G. Ord-Hume and rendered into usable spruce to enable him to build a Luton Minor while the other was eventually burnt. Also, during 1949/50, many RAF-surplus Miles Magisters were delivered for future conversion to Hawk Trainers for civilian use but in the event most were broken up, burnt or sold abroad.

A couple of Miles M.14A Hawk Trainer 3s earmarked for the British civil register pictured on arrival at Elstree c. 1949. On the left is G-ALNX, still bearing its RAF serial number L8211 and sporting a blind flying hood behind the rear cockpit. In the event this 'Maggie' was never converted and was scrapped at Elstree in October 1952. The other 'Maggie' is G-ALNY/L8075 which, together with G-ALOF/N5430, was never converted. Both went up in smoke during the Elstree Flying Club's Guy Fawkes night celebrations on 5 November 1953! *(Arthur W.J.G. Ord-Hume)*

Miles M.14A Hawk Trainer 3 G-ALOE, formerly N3926 in the RAF, did make it and received its Certificate of Airworthiness at Elstree in December 1949. In 1952 this 'Maggie' was sold in Belgium and became OO-ACH. *(Arthur W.J.G. Ord-Hume)*

4 Years of Peace

By 1950 the postwar flurry of activity had died down and most of the resident charter companies had ceased trading or moved away. The roofs of the wartime hangars, which were still owned by the Ministry of Supply, had deteriorated to the point where they were almost non-existent, being made from ungalvanised steel sheets. Added to this, LAMS' staff had been given notice and the aerodrome was in danger of closing down. Fortunately John Houlder, who owned a shipping company and had a Miles Messenger hangared at Elstree, was persuaded to keep it going for a few weeks until Lord Aldenham, the ground landlord, could find

This photograph of Elstree taken in 1951 shows the aerodrome in the doldrums and practically deserted, with just three Austers and a Fairchild Argus in the open. The short-lived blister hangar, once located at the top of the picture, has been removed to make way for the Hilfield Reservoir. The field at top left was completely submerged shortly after this photograph was taken. (Aerofilms)

a professional manager. His negotiations were unsuccessful and he eventually accepted John Houlder's earlier offer. This arrangement was acceptable to the Ministry of Supply and John Houlder set up the Montclare Shipping Company to run the aerodrome, which it still does today. His first job was to purchase and re-roof the hangars and take out the first of several ground leases from the Aldenham Estate. At the same time, a relatively steep slope on the north side of the main hangar was used as a tip for rubble to provide a level apron area.

When LAMS ceased trading in 1950 its three Autocrats were purchased for £300 each by John Houlder to enable him to start up the Elstree Flying Club. The Air Schools Group, which comprised Wolverhampton Aviation and Derby Aviation, subsequently acquired this in April 1952, but it retained its title. The Air Schools Group had been formed in 1938 at Derby (Burnaston) to operate flying schools for the RAF and trained more than 14,000 pilots during the war. As well as the Autocrats, the Group originally operated Miles Hawk Trainers and a Miles Gemini at Elstree, finished in a two-tone blue paint scheme. However, Elstree Flying Club continued to trade under its own name until 1960 when it became the London School of Flying and was eventually taken over by the Cabair Group. Air Schools and Wolverhampton Aviation were absorbed into the parent Derby Aviation which in turn became Derby Airways and subsequently British Midland Airways (now BMI International).

This photograph of the Elstree Flying Club's fleet at Elstree was taken on 26 July 1953. Nearest the camera is Miles M.14A Hawk Trainer 3 G-AJJI, built in 1940 as T9698 for the RAF and written off at Elstree on 19 August 1956. Next to G-AJJI is Miles Hawk Trainer 3 G-AHNW, complete with rear cockpit blind flying hood, written off at Elstree on 2 June 1957. The three Auster J.1 Autocrats are G-AGXT, G-AHAP and G-AGVN. *(Photoflight Ltd)*

The all silver Miles M.65 Gemini 3C G-ALCS was owned by aerodrome licensee and leaseholder John Houlder and based at Elstree for many years. Purchased as a heap of components from the Miles factory the aircraft was assembled by Ron Paine at Wolverhampton in 1950 and, fitted with more powerful de Havilland Gipsy Major 10 engines, became the first Series 3 Gemini. Flown all over Europe by its owner G-ALCS was finally withdrawn from use in 1972. Note the row of poplar trees on the runway approach in the background. These trees feature prominently in many of the photographs in this book. Sadly they had to be removed in the 1970s as they were causing a major obstruction to landing aircraft. *(RTR)*

A pilot's view of the approach to Elstree Aerodrome's grass strip, albeit a trifle too high! The uninviting water of Hilfield Reservoir makes a last-minute overshoot somewhat undesirable! Use of the grass strip was discontinued in the 1970s. This photograph was taken in 1956, the year that the reservoir was completed. Hilfield Reservoir and the adjacent Aldenham Reservoir have their uses – in certain light conditions they present an unmistakable feature to visiting pilots! *(The Aeroplane)*

Pictured on 26 July 1953 are members of the Elstree Flying Club's staff. From left to right; chief engineer Ernie Chick, who had his own aircraft maintenance business – Light Planes Maintenance Services – at Elstree for more than twenty-five years, A.D. Pickup, club secretary G.E. Hilder, chief flying instructor David F. Ogilvy and A. Noyes. *(Photoflight Ltd)*

A vic of Elstree Flying Club aircraft comprising Auster J.1 Autocrat G-AHAP, Miles M.65 Gemini G-AJTL and Miles M.14A Hawk Trainer 3 G-AKUA, flown by club instructors over Elstree Aerodrome in mid-1956. The club's fleet at this time comprised four Autocrats, four Miles M.14A Hawk Trainers and a Miles Gemini, all run by Derby Aviation. The colour scheme for all Club aircraft was light blue with dark blue trim and lettering. David Ogilvy was manager and chief flying instructor. Flying rates were £4 4s an hour on the Auster and £4 2s on the Miles Hawk Trainer. Later in the year G-AOSY, the first DHC1 Chipmunk to enter service with a civilian flying club in this country, joined the fleet, the rate for which was £5 5s an hour. *(The Aeroplane)*

Arthur W.J.G. Ord-Hume remembers that in the early days before Air Schools took over, the Elstree Flying Club held numerous parties to celebrate, among other things, either the least number of members facing prosecution for low flying, or the most! He also recalls that on one occasion club members tied the windsock to a length of string and hauled it tight at right angles to the runway on a still weather day, just to see how a particular pilot coped with the very strong, but non-existent, cross wind on landing! The days of the United Services Flying Club were rife with misdemeanours and it was reliably reported by several people that Dr Graham Humby flew an Auster through the main hangar, but no witnesses to the event can be found!

For several years during the 1950s Elstree Flying Club was the busiest in the country and won the Lennox Boyd Trophy for the most efficient flying club for three or four consecutive years. Later their four Chipmunks each achieved more flying hours in a year than any other club/school aircraft.

In late 1949 the Colne Valley Water Board purchased part of the south-western area of the aerodrome to incorporate into the new Hilfield Reservoir and this necessitated the removal of the blister hangar and a temporary dwelling occupied by the ground engineer, John 'Tubby' Simpson. A feature of the aerodrome in the early years was an avenue of tall poplar trees along the Aldenham Road boundary, at the eastern end of the main runway. Unfortunately, these caused an obstruction to landing aircraft and the tops had to be lopped regularly in the 1940s and '50s. They were eventually removed altogether.

In the early 1950s there were two maintenance organisations based at the aerodrome, Simpsons Aeroservices run by 'Tubby' Simpson, the former Chief Engineer for LAMS, and Light Plane Maintenance Services under Ernie Chick. In 1955, Derby Aviation came up with an interesting proposal for Elstree. Their idea was to use its newly acquired Miles Marathons to operate a service from Derby to the Isle of Wight via Elstree but this did not materialise.

This 1972 aerial view of Elstree Aerodrome shows it populated almost entirely by tin aeroplanes, mostly American, with not a wooden machine in sight. The London School of Flying offices and classrooms, occupied today by Cabair and others, were erected by the LSF in 1964 at a cost of more than £20,000. *(RTR)*

A company very much in evidence during the 1950s and 60s was Hunting Aerosurveys which operated a diverse fleet of aircraft including a Douglas DC3 much adorned with aerials for carrying out geophysical survey work overseas, Percival Princes, a DH89A Dragon Rapide and an Airspeed Oxford.

Some modest development took place in the 1960s, the first since the wartime expansion. Firstly, a new control tower and signals area was commissioned by David Ogilvy in 1960 to replace an earlier wooden structure and this heralded the introduction of radio communications. Prior to this Aldis Lamps or Very pistols were used to pass instructions to aircraft. Next, in 1964, a single-storey office block was built to the west of the main hangar, which is now used mainly by Cabair and an assortment of aviation-related companies. Lastly, a new 'Coseley' hangar was constructed in 1969 for Samuelson Aviation, which was subsequently used by a Piper agent in the 1970s, later by Cabair Helicopters and currently by Firecrest Aviation.

Polyfoto Air Taxi Services began operations in December 1963 with one Piper Apache which was kept busy transporting the rich and famous. These included film stars, pop stars and TV personalities, including Elizabeth Taylor, Bing Crosby, Bob Monkhouse and David Frost. In October 1965 Polyfoto took over the London School of Flying (LSF) and changed its name to London Aviation, but the LSF continued to operate under its own name with its large fleet of Piper Cherokees and DHC Chipmunks. Presswork became one of London's specialities, carrying camera crews and reporters all over the country, as well as newsreel film to TV centres. London Aviation negotiated agreements with several international airlines whereby one of the company's air taxis would meet incoming passengers and then fly them to their required destination – perhaps a small airstrip or airfield not served by a scheduled service. The company also became one of the founder members of the Air Taxi Operators' Association.

In April 1971 another change in title took place when Cabair bought out London Aviation. This company had started as an air taxi/charter operator at Fairoaks in late 1968 with one Piper Apache and soon moved its base to Heathrow, where it was the only air taxi firm at the main London airport at that time. When it purchased London Aviation, Cabair transferred all operations to Elstree where it is still very much in evidence today as a major user of the aerodrome and operator of the London School of Flying.

Another 1960s charter/air taxi company which formed at Elstree was Skywork which traded as Lennard Aviation and began operations during September 1964 with one Piper Twin Commanche. However, this aircraft was operated under the name of its parent company Allwear Trading Ltd. Its stay at Elstree was very short as it moved to Stapleford Tawney on 1 April 1965. It reverted to Skywork and eventually ceased operations in 1975.

Companies that arrived in the 1970s included Rimmer Air Taxi Service, which commenced operations in 1973 with a Piper Aztec leased from Cabair. An associate company, Rimmer Aviation, was a main Piper agent as well as being responsible for the construction and sale of the remaining Beagle Pup airframes which have long been a familiar sight at Elstree.

For nearly 20 years volunteer pilots flew from Elstree on behalf of St John Ambulance delivering organs for transplantation, but these flights ceased in 1991 when chartered aircraft were used.

5 Elstree in the Twenty-first Century

Elstree is the nearest general aviation aerodrome to London's West End and City. It is conveniently placed for the Jubilee underground line at Stanmore (4 miles) and the Thameslink main line at Elstree & Borehamwood, or Radlett, both about 3 miles away. It is used by business people, private owners and for training. Currently the two resident flying schools are the London School of Flying, part of the Cabair Group, and Firecrest Aviation. Very few vintage aircraft are based at Elstree, due mainly to the lack of a grass strip and hangar space. Customs are available on 24 hours prior notice and runway lighting is provided, although night operations have to be booked in advance. Cabair's maintenance organisation occupies the two Super Robin hangars while private owners and maintenance companies use the 'R' type main hangar. Despite the main hangar's large size there

Various 'spamcans' in front of the main hangar, no. 5, October 2000. This is a rare example of an 'R' type hangar, designed for the Ministry of Aircraft Production and erected at several UK airfields where production and/or maintenance was being carried out. They had the advantage over the similar T2 and Bellman hangars of the roof structure being able to carry a runway track for a chain and hoist to assist with the removal of engines and other items of heavy equipment. It was built in 1942 to enable Fairfield Aviation to modify/repair Vickers Wellingtons and is now used by private owners and maintenance organisations. *(GRP)*

As Elstree Aerodrome entered the twenty-first century its popularity showed no signs of decline. The layout of the buildings has changed little in forty years, though additional taxiways and parking spaces have proliferated recently. *(Pete Stevens)*

Elstree Aerodrome

The only new hangar to be provided at Elstree since the war is this 'Coseley' example built in 1969 for Samuelson Aviation. It can accommodate four aeroplanes and two helicopters and is currently occupied by Firecrest Aviation, one of the two training organisations based at the aerodrome. *(GRP)*

is still insufficient hangar space and many aircraft have to be parked outside. The two pre-war timber hangars collapsed in the late 1960s and the land on which they were situated no longer forms part of the active aerodrome.

The concrete runway laid down in 1942 continued to be fully used up to 1950 when, with the departure of the previously based large multi-engined aircraft, it was clear that the full length was no longer required. Maintenance of approximately 600ft of the western extremity was then terminated and a line was painted across the runway at that point, which happened to coincide with the boundary between Bushey UDC and Watford RDC. A narrow strip down the centre was retained for use in an emergency. Today the runway is overlaid with asphalt and the length normally available for take-offs and landings is 2,152ft (656m).

Elstree is still considered rather difficult, a problem which goes back to its origins in the 1930s. While the overhead power lines are no longer a limiting factor, as the single runway has been aligned to avoid them, there is still a significant slope on the relatively short strip. The approach from the east to runway 26 is over the Haberdashers' School and from the west over trees to runway 08. There has been long standing opposition from noise-sensitive local residents who complain regularly about the nuisance caused by overflying aircraft but the operator does as much as possible to ameliorate the situation. For example, visitors are required to make a straight-in approach from 4 miles out and circuits are for training only and are changed every hour.

Some 160 aircraft are currently based at Elstree, of which an unusually high number are twin-engined types. The aerodrome handles in the region of 60,000 movements annually, of which approximately 45,000 are training flights. The current lease on the aerodrome expires in 2006.

On the left of this picture is a pair of 'Super Robin' hangars which were built by the Ministry of Aircraft Production around 1942 for Fairfield Aviation to repair and assemble smaller aircraft like the Westland Lysander and Miles Master. They were originally built as two separate hangars, nos 3 and 4, but were later opened up to provide one large building. They were re-roofed in 1950 by Montclare Shipping Company following acquisition from the Ministry of Supply. These hangars have been used by a number of companies since the war including Simpsons Aeroservices and Hunting Aerosurveys. They are currently home to Cabair's maintenance operation. Montclare Shipping Company, the operators of the aerodrome, uses the low white building in the foreground as a store. *(GRP)*

Interior view of the 'Super Robin' hangars showing to good effect the space made available by opening up the two originally separate buildings. An assortment of American-built singles can be seen undergoing maintenance by Cabair. *(GRP)*

This photograph taken in October 2000 shows the current control tower which was built in 1960 to replace an earlier postwar timber building (seen in the photos on pages 78, 99 and 109). Before and during the war a wooden structure attached to hangar no. 1 was used for flying control. Until the arrival of radio with the new tower, communication was by Very pistol or Aldis lamp. A signal square was at one time laid out in front of the tower but is no longer used. *(GRP)*

Another view of the main 'R' type hangar showing the assortment of single-storey buildings along its south side which are used for various aviation related activities, some having direct access from the hangar. This hangar was purchased by Montclare Shipping Company in 1950 from the Ministry of Supply and re-roofed. *(GRP)*

This building was constructed for the London School of Flying in 1964 to replace a smaller building situated near the front of the main hangar. The Cabair Group, operators of the LSF, currently occupies it together with other aviation-related organisations. With the exception of the 'Coseley' hangar built in 1969, this office block was the last development at Elstree. *(GRP)*

Rear view of hangar No. 5 showing the apron area on which the mortal remains of HP Halifax G-AHZM languished for four years between 1946 and 1950, when it was finally broken up. Part of this end of the hangar is currently partitioned-off to provide a maintenance facility for Cabair Helicopters. *(GRP)*

72 Elstree Aerodrome

This 1961 aerial photograph, looking east, shows clearly the boundaries of Elstree Aerodrome, with Hilfield Reservoir to the right. Hilfield Castle, built in 1805, can be seen at bottom right. At the eastern end of the runway, amidst the woodland at the top of the picture, can be seen the newly built Haberdashers' Aske's school adjacent to Aldenham House. The dreaded line of electricity pylons can just be discerned running parallel and two fields to the left of the runway, extending from the western outskirts of Borehamwood, at top left, to the bottom of the photograph. The photograph was taken in winter from an Auster and a Miles Gemini can be spotted midway down the runway. *(RTR)*

6 Private Residents

In recent years Elstree Aerodrome's resident population has peaked at around 160 aircraft. Since it opened in 1934 the aerodrome's proximity to central and north London has attracted many hundreds of private owners. The following pages illustrate only a small percentage of private residents.

After a day out Elstree-based Taylorcraft Auster 4 G-ANHU, flaps down, returns home one late summer's afternoon in 1959. Owned at the time by E. Richards this smart blue and silver Auster was sold in Spain in 1964 and became EC-AXR. *(RTR)*

Robinson Redwing G-ABNX, built in 1932, had been stored in one of Elstree's hangars since about 1944. It was re-discovered, completely hidden by junk, by Arthur W.J.G. Ord-Hume in 1948. This photograph was taken after the rubbish had been cleared and shortly before G-ABNX was removed to the ULAA's blister hangar to the west of the aerodrome. At the time of writing G-ABNX was still airworthy. *(EJR)*

Aeronca 100 G-AEVT was built in 1938 and rebuilt after the war by Arthur W.J.G Ord-Hume and Paul Simpson at Pinner during 1948-49. Once airworthy the Aeronca was based for a while at Elstree until it crashed at Loughborough in July 1950. In the background at left is the Beech D-17S G-AJJJ and just visible is Auster 5 G-AKOT. *(EJR)*

1938 Miles M.11 Whitney Straight G-AFGK based at Elstree in the late 1950s and 1960s was doped grey overall with red trim and owned by the Aldenham Private Flying Group. In 2003 the aircraft was owned by Stan Reynolds Ltd at Wetaskiwin, Alberta and registered CF-FGK. *(RTR)*

Cyril Croxon and Ron Lane's red and cream 1939 DH90 Moth Minor G-AFNI flying circuits and bumps at Elstree in 1959. Originally built in 1939 with an open cockpit G-AFNI was converted to a coupe configuration at Panshanger in 1954 and subsequently flown extensively around Europe. Having not flown since 1967 this Moth Minor was being rebuilt in 2003. *(RTR)*

C. Nepean Bishop, his tongue sticking out with concentration, taking off from Elstree on 3 July 1949 in Miles M.14A Hawk Trainer 3 G-AIUA while being photographed by EJR from Auster Autocrat G-AGXT. This 'Maggie' was later on the strength of Elstree-based Air Schools during the 1950s until retired in 1959, when it was acquired by Borehamwood butcher Sid Aarons. The 'Maggie' was cleaned up for air racing – see below – and flown into third place in the 1961 King's Cup air race by Elstree CFI W.H. 'Bill' Bailey at an average speed of 133mph. *(EJR)*

Sid Aarons taxiing in during an early test flight from Elstree in 1960. Note the fabric strips sealing the enclosed rear cockpit and the trousered spats, normally discarded from working Maggies, but replaced to add a few extra knots. The aircraft was doped white with lurid pink wings and lower fuselage. Sid Aarons flew 'UA in the 1961 and 1962 King's Cup events. Following a crash at Roborough on 26 September 1965 the remains have been in storage for many years. *(RTR)*

The dark blue two-seat Taylorcraft Plus D G-AIXB, previously LB378 with the RAF, pictured at Elstree with Eddie Riding in 1948. G-AIXB was sold in Rhodesia in February 1956 and became YP-YNM. *(EJR)*

Benes-Mraz Sokol M.1C G-AIXN, built in 1947 by Automobilov Zavody at Chocen, Czechoslovakia and registered OK-BHA, was owned for many years by A.R. 'Tiny' Pilgrim and kept at Elstree. During the late 1950s this sole British-registered example spent some years at Elstree on extended rebuild. G-AIXN is currently airworthy. *(RTR)*

Piper L-4H Cub G-AJBE outside the main hangar in slush at Elstree in 1947. In May 1948 this Cub was re-registered G-AKNC because its earlier registration had already been applied to a Handley Page Halifax. The Cub was later registered NC6400N to the American Embassy Flying Club. Spitfire II G-AHZI can be seen lurking inside the hangar. Note the wooden control tower in the background. *(EJR)*

A.R. 'Tiny' Pilgrim's Beechcraft D-17S G-AJJJ at Elstree in 1948. This 'Staggerwing' was one of 30 C-43s supplied under Lend-Lease and flew with the Royal Navy during the war as FZ432. In 1952 G-AJJJ was sold in Australia and became VH-MJE. *(EJR)*

J.V. Heriz-Smith's Auster J.5B Autocar G-AJYN was the third built and was based at Elstree from March 1950 for several years until sold in Spain as EC-ANK in 1957. It is pictured at Elstree shortly after it was delivered from Rearsby. *(Arthur W.J.G.Ord-Hume)*

Miles M.38 Messenger 4A G-ALBR, owned by Tom Hayhow, pictured shortly before it crashed into trees immediately after taking off from Elstree on 2 July 1949 – see page 160. *(EJR)*

Taylorcraft Auster 5 G-ALBW was used by Elstree-based Photoflight Ltd for aerial photography during the 1950s. On 24 July 1952 the pilot/photographer was returning to Elstree from a sortie in the West Country when the aircraft dived into the ground at Booker. At the subsequent inquiry it was revealed that when not using the vertical camera installed in the rear of the cockpit the pilot weighted down the cover over the hole in the floor with a brick. It was concluded that the cover had come adrift and fumes from the engine had passed up through the hole and rendered the pilot unconscious. *(EJR)*

1951 Auster J.5F Aiglet G-AMMS, later converted to J.5K standard, was once owned by entertainer Jimmy Edwards and famously took part in the 1952 SBAC show at Farnborough, demonstrated by Auster supremo Ranald Porteous. The Aiglet later passed to Keith Ewart and was used by co-author Richard Riding for aerial photography throughout the 1960s. Later 'MS became the subject for the Auster Club's logo and was still extant in 2003. *(RTR)*

Red and white de Havilland DH82A Tiger Moth G-AOIM was based at Elstree and owned by Mike Fallon. On 25 May 1967 it was badly damaged when it ground-looped spectacularly after landing at Elstree. The Tiger was repaired and in 2003 was alive and well and living in the Cardigan area. *(RTR)*

John Duer flying the North Middlesex Flying Group's red two-seat Auster 5J G-APJM in the Elstree circuit on 1 August 1960. On 27 May 1961 the same pilot was flying G-APJM across the English Channel when an engine problem forced him to ditch close to the Varne Lightship. John Duer got wet but was otherwise unscathed; the Auster is presumably still lurking at the bottom of the sea. *(RTR)*

Airspeed Oxford I G-AJGR, registered to Hunting Aerosurveys Ltd in July 1947, was based at Elstree until it was scrapped in 1952. *(RTR Collection)*

Eddie Wild flying Hunting Aerosurveys' DH89A Dragon Rapide G-AIYR in the Elstree circuit on 13 January 1961. In recent years this venerable Rapide has operated pleasure flights with Classic Wings out of Duxford during the summer season. *(RTR)*

Seen here at Elstree in about 1960 is Percival P.50 Prince F-BJAI/G-AMLW in the colours of Société Protection Aéroportée at the time it was used for airfield radar calibration duties. *(RTR)*

Hunting Aerosurveys Ltd operated several Percival Princes, most of which regularly called in to Elstree for maintenance. Two of the company's long-nosed Survey Princes are seen here at Elstree in November 1953. In the foreground is P.54 Survey Prince G-ALRY pictured on its return from survey work in East Africa, with Prince 4D G-AMOT behind. The latter had just returned from RAF Shawbury giving Magnetometer crew training prior to leaving for Assam. *(RTR Collection)*

Huntings' Prince G-ALRY appeared at Elstree in several different registrations and is seen here as F-BJAJ in about 1959 (below) and VP-KNN. During the 1950s this Prince flew extensive survey tours in Kuwait, Persia, Siam and Turkey, returning to Elstree every so often for maintenance. The sound of the Prince's noisy Alvis Leonides engines always attracted a crowd of onlookers to witness it taking off. *(RTR)*

Engine problems permitting, the Bellamy-Currie Wot G-APWT was flown by members of the Elstree-based M.P.M. Flying Group during the 1960s. It is seen here making a rare self-propelled return to Elstree. Built and first flown in 1959 G-APWT was later fitted experimentally with a 60hp Rover gas turbine engine and dubbed the 'Jet Wot'. In 1962 the Wot reverted to its original Mikron power. G-APWT was sold in America in 1975. *(RTR)*

Czechoslovakian Aero 45 G-APRR, formerly OK-KFQ in its native land, was registered in Britain in 1959. Much later it resided at Elstree and was owned by C. 'Jack' Reid. Powered by two 110hp Letadlovy M-332 engines the Aero 45 was noted for the excellent field of view from its cockpit. Note the ancient Elstree Aerodrome bowser lurking in the background. *(RTR)*

During a period between 1960 and 1962 a succession of Austers arrived from exotic lands in the hands of one John Tussaud. On arrival each would disappear into the main hangar for weeks at a time to emerge eventually as freshly registered as-new aircraft. The first to arrive, in early 1960, was Auster J.1B Aiglet VP-SZZ, with a Somaliland registration crudely applied and looking tired after an obviously long journey. This Auster later emerged as G-ARBM and was sold to local private owner Colin Winter. In September 1962 the Auster was sold in Ireland and became EI-AMO. *(RTR)*

Another Auster brought in to Elstree by John Tussaud was J.5G Autocar AP-AHJ. An enormous tank leaving barely enough room for the pilot took up most of the cockpit. Fitted out for aerial spraying the tank was presumably filled with fuel for the long flight to Elstree. After several weeks work this aircraft emerged into the daylight as G-ARKG, minus the tank, and was sold to the Norfolk and Norwich Aero Club in August 1961. *(RTR)*

The next arrival crept in after a heavy snowfall in early 1962 bearing the temporary registrations AP-AHI on one side of the rudder and G-ARUT on the other. The records say that this Auster J.5G Autocar was originally AP-AJW and subsequently became AP-AHI. In May the transformed aircraft was registered G-ARUT and was sold to H.E. Smead and resided at Elstree until it was written off following a forced landing at nearby Barnet on 13 August 1965. *(RTR)*

Tipsy T.66 Nipper 2 G-ARBP was delivered to Lympne from Belgium and flown from there to Elstree by David Greenland on 15 July 1960. On arrival it was flown by all and sundry, including most of the CPL students, who found it great fun to fly. In this photograph CPL student Francis Newton calls 'switches on' while engineer Derek Cobb stoops to swing the tiny prop. The yard and a half of string hanging on to the starboard wing is co-author Richard Riding. *(Brian Turpin)*

In 1960, after parting with his faithful old Miles Gemini G-ALCS, John Houlder acquired the Cessna 310C G-ARBI, formerly N2611C in the USA. This 310 was flown extensively all over Europe and was a regular visitor to Samadan, St Moritz. After John Houlder sold the two-tone blue and white Cessna it was written off on 2 August 1972. *(RTR)*

The ill-fated Saab 91A Safir G-ARFX at Elstree in 1962, shortly before its fatal crash – see pages 162 and 163 The all-metal four-seat Safir 91A was designed as a trainer and was produced in Sweden from 1945. Powered by a 145hp DH Gipsy Major 10 Mk 2 engine the aircraft sat unusually low to the ground, allowing easy access. G-ARFX was previously registered PH-UEC in Holland. *(RTR)*

Piper PA-23 Apache 150 G-ARHJ pictured shortly before it was involved in Elstree's worst flying accident. On 27 January 1968, after sitting in the hangar unflown for some considerable time, the Apache took off on a demonstration flight with a potential customer. Immediately after take-off the port engine failed and the aircraft veered to the left and crashed into the adjacent reservoir. All three occupants were killed. The subsequent accident investigation attributed the engine failure to water in the fuel, caused by condensation in the fuel tank. *(RTR)*

G-ARHE was one of a batch of Forney F. 1A Aircoupes imported into the UK in 1960. Registered to Thurston Engineering Ltd in February 1961 and based at Stapleford Tawney, Essex together with several of its brethren, the red and white Aircoupe is pictured during a visit to Elstree in March the same year. On 4 June 1965 the Aircoupe was written off when it crashed at Kelvedon Hatch. *(Brian Turpin)*

Co-author Richard Riding snapped during an aerial photographic sortie in Keith Ewart's Beagle A. 109 Airedale G-ASAH, c. 1965. *(Howard Grey)*

Nord 1002 Pingouin II F-BGKI was registered G-ASTG in November 1964 to the Nipper Flying Group and was mostly flown by Dave Vince of Elstree-based Airline Instruments and former London School of Flying CFI David Greenland. In 2003 this aircraft was in a dismantled state at Duxford. *(RTR)*

Opposite: After selling his Auster Aiglet G-AMMS in 1964 Keith Ewart acquired Beagle A. 109 Airedale G-ASAH. He had been angling after the Airedale prototype G-ARKE, for obvious reasons, but had to settle for an early production model. Resembling an Auster Autocar with a tricycle undercarriage and a swept fin the Airedale was built like a battleship. With the rear passenger door removed it made an ideal camera-ship and this blue and white Airedale was used by Richard Riding for aerial photographic work until the arrival of the owner's Cessna 337 G-AWKE a few years later. G-ASAH was written off on 23 July 1972. *(RTR)*

Keith Ewart eventually purchased an aircraft with a personalised registration. Seen here is his blue and white Cessna 337 C Super Skymaster G-AWKE on a local flight from Elstree on 20 February 1971. In addition to being used by Richard Riding for aerial photographic work 'KE made regular business flights to Europe between 1968 and 1976 flown by the owner. It was also used for life-saving flights ferrying human organs on behalf of the St John Ambulance Air Wing, mostly flown by W.H. 'Bill' Bailey who flew around 75 such flights. After Ewart sold 'KE Cessna 337s were banned from Elstree on account of the high noise level of the 210hp Continental engines. Sadly G-AWKE was written off on 28 April 1976 when it crashed onto cloud-covered Jaizkibel Mountain while trying to land at San Sebastian, Spain. *(RTR)*

Opposite: Surrounded by scores of seemingly giant London School of Flying Grumman types W.H. 'Bill' Bailey taxis out to air test the diminutive Quickie G-BHUK early in 1981. Built in a year by a London-based group the aircraft was lost in a crash on 22 April the same year. *(RTR)*

John Houlder's Aero Commander 680E G-AWOE, formerly N3844C, was first registered in August 1968 and is seen at Elstree shortly after delivery. Later painted black overall G-AWOE has remained in John Houlder's ownership for more than thirty years. *(RTR)*

Capital Radio's Flying Eye aircraft have been based at Elstree for many years and pictured here is Plane Talking's Grumman American GA-7 Cougar G-FLII, advertising Capital Gold 1548 AM. Built in 1977 this Cougar was previously registered G-GRAC. *(GRP)*

Graham Hill's first Piper Aztec N6094Y, bought with the prize money he received for winning the 1966 Indianapolis 500, seen shortly after its arrival at Elstree in July 1966. Hill replaced this aircraft with Piper PA-23 Aztec D N6645Y in 1970. On the night of 28 November 1975 he and five team mates were returning to Elstree from Marseilles. Just 3 miles from touchdown they ran into fog and the Aztec crashed on Arkley Golf Course and burst into flames – all six occupants were killed. *(RTR)*

7 Giving Them Wings

Since 1946 many hundreds of people have learnt to fly and gained private and commercial pilots' licences with Elstree's various flying clubs and schools.

Elstree Flying Club, run by Derby Aviation Ltd, received its first DHC1 Chipmunk, G-AOSY, at the end of 1956. Chipmunks G-AOSO and G-AOSN soon followed and all three aircraft are seen flying in formation past Hilfield Reservoir early in 1959. (Derby Aerosurveys)

During the 1950s the Derby Aviation-operated Elstree Flying Club had several Elstree-based Miles M.14A Hawk Trainer 3s on strength as PPL training aircraft. Here David Ogilvy and W.H. 'Bill' Bailey are flying G-AKUA from Elstree in about 1956. This 'Maggie' crashed at Burnaston, Derby on 21 July 1957. *(Via Michael Stroud)*

This photograph of a line-up of three Elstree Flying Club Miles M.14A Hawk Trainer 3s was taken in about 1956 and shows W.H. 'Bill' Bailey in the foreground explaining the purpose of wheel chocks to a pupil. Behind, standing on the wing of G-AKKR, is David Ogilvy briefing another student. Note the blind-flying hood on the rear cockpit. *(Photoflight, via Michael Stroud)*

Pictured here in 1959 is Elstree Flying Club Miles M. 14A Hawk Trainer 3 G-AKPG, formerly L5925 with the RAF. Derby Aviation replaced its 'Maggie' fleet with DHC1 Chipmunks and by the end of 1959 had phased out the Hawk Trainers. G-AKPG was written off in November 1964. *(RTR)*

Auster J.1 Autocrat G-AGTP, together with Autocrat G-AGXT, were part and parcel of the Elstree landscape throughout the 1950s and 1960s. In addition to charter and training work Derby Aerosurveys used both aircraft for photographic work. Originally powered by a 100hp Blackburn Cirrus Minor engine 'TP was upgraded in about 1961 to J.1N standard and fitted with a 120hp D.H. Gipsy Major 1c; a belly-mounted long-range fuel tank was added during the conversion. After flying many thousand hours 'TP was finally written off in May 1978. *(RTR)*

During the early 1960s the London School of Flying used two Ansons for twin-engine flight training. The first arrival was the veteran Avro Anson I G-AMDA, built as N4877 for the RAF in 1938. Purchased by Derby Aviation in the early 1950s G-AMDA was installed with a continuous-strip vertical camera and a Speedomax magnetometer recorder and bird, the latter towed on a line in flight. During 1955–6 the Anson patrolled lonely 90-mile beats on a geophysical survey of England covering 11,000 square miles carried out by Canadian Aero Service Ltd in association with Derby Aviation Ltd. From about 1959 the ancient Anson was based at Elstree and was employed by the London School of Flying as a twin-trainer in addition to carrying out aerial survey for the route of the proposed M4 motorway and the new town at Basingstoke. Known by students as the 'cloth bomber', G-AMDA served as a stopgap until the arrival of the 1946 Avro 19 Series 2 G-AGWE in 1962. CPL students elsewhere were training on modern nose-wheel aircraft such as the early Piper and Cessna twins! G-AMDA was acquired by Skyfame Ltd and flown at Staverton in RAF colours until it was damaged while landing there in November 1972. The Anson is currently preserved at Duxford in non-flying condition. *(RTR)*

With tailplane oscillating alarmingly the Anson's Cheetah engines are run up prior to another CPL training flight from Elstree in 1962. *(RTR)*

A tribute to X-ray Tango

Auster Autocrat G-AGXT was first registered in 1946 to LAMS and was destined to spend many years based at Elstree. Early in its life this aircraft achieved some notoriety when it was involved in the famous Stanley Setty murder case. In October 1949 Setty, a 46-year-old Palestinian, went missing after receiving a roll of more than 200 £5 notes in payment for a car deal. Two weeks after he was reported missing a grey bundle containing a human torso was found floating on the mud flats at Tillingham in Essex by a farm labourer. Subsequent investigation by a pathologist revealed that death had been the result of stab wounds to the chest but, because every bone in the torso had been crushed, it was assumed that the torso had been dropped from a great height some time after death. Later, after details were published in the press, the chief engineer of the United Services Flying Club at Elstree revealed to police that on 5 October one Donald Hume had hired G-AGXT for the afternoon. He had paid for the hire with £5 notes and had told the engineer that he was flying to Southend. When forensic examination of G-AGXT revealed bloodstains behind the pilot's seat, Hume claimed that he had been paid by two individuals to dump a parcel into the sea. He had driven it to Southend, to where he had flown the Auster, and then flew the parcel out to sea and dumped it. Though Hume was charged with Setty's murder the jury failed to agree upon a verdict. At a second trial Hume pleaded guilty to being an accessory to the fact and was sentenced to 12 years' imprisonment.

As an aside co-author Richard Riding's father flew G-AGXT from Elstree to Hastings and back on 15 October 1949 and was interviewed by the police during the course of their inquiries only because he flew the aircraft on a regular basis. Ten years later Richard began clocking up many hours in 'XT taking aerial photographs for Elstree-based Derby Aerosurveys.

In June 1956 G-AGXT celebrated its tenth birthday and 5,000 flying hours with the club by towing a banner declaring, 'I am ten today'. An oversize birthday cake was cut and a French television actress adorned the Auster's propeller with a bouquet.

An early photograph of Auster J.1 Autocrat G-AGXT at Elstree in United Services Flying Club colours – the logo on the fin was designed by a club member.
(RTR Collection)

Trainee commercial pilot Roger Wilson is seen here in the left-hand seat of the London School of Flying's Auster Autocrat G-AGXT on a flight from Elstree to Denham in July 1959. In the right-hand seat is instructor Janet L. Ferguson who that month had taken part in the *Daily Mail* Blériot Anniversary Race. The race between London and Paris was held between 13 and 23 July 1959 to commemorate Blériot's crossing of the English Channel fifty years earlier. After flying in to Enghien Moiselles Janet covered the last 18 miles on a borrowed bicycle! She was one of Britain's greatest but unsung aviatrixes, spending most of her adult life instructing and ferrying, interspersed with the odd air race. After a period instructing at Denham in the early 1950s she became an instructor at Elstree in 1959 and later embarked upon a long career ferrying aircraft for Peter Nock. See page 168 for a more recognisable view of Janet. *(RTR)*

This photograph shows Elstree veteran Auster Autocrat G-AGXT about to be carted back to its birthplace at Auster's Rearsby aerodrome for rebuild after a lady pilot nosed it over while landing on the grass strip. Note the Auster logo on the lorry's passenger door. The Auster returned re-engined with a D.H. Gipsy Major 1c engine and greatly enhanced performance. Although G-AGXT crashed at Bickmarsh, Warwickshire on 7 June 1969 following an engine failure the airframe has been under rebuild for many years and it may yet fly again. *(RTR)*

DHC1 Chipmunk G-APOE joined the London School of Flying fleet in late 1968 and is seen here in later LSF two-tone blue livery during a rather high landing approach at Elstree. G-APOE was sold in America in 1970. *(RTR)*

London School of Flying CPL students at Elstree in 1959. Left to right: Tom Phethean (half-hidden), -?-, -?-, -?-, 'Jock' Campbell, Dave Antrobus (founder of Northern Executive Aviation Ltd in 1961), Roger Healey (killed in Anglian Air Charter's Auster 5 G-AKOT pleasure flying at Gorleston, Norfolk on 9 September 1962 just weeks after getting his CPL) and CFI John Schooling. *(The Aeroplane)*

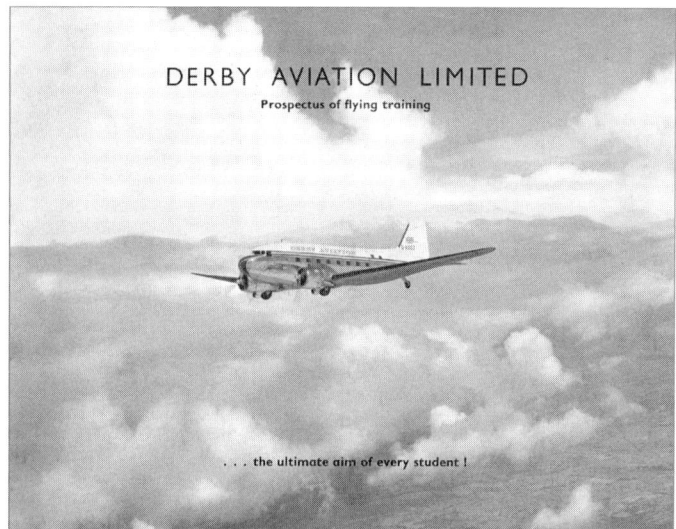

Front cover of Derby Aviation's Elstree-based flying training prospectus from about 1958 featuring the company's Douglas DC-3 Dakota IV G-AOGZ beneath which appears the line '. . . the ultimate aim of every student!' In 1958 the cost of acquiring a private pilot's licence was between £140 and £170. The cost of a commercial pilot's licence was £1,000, including ground-training costs. *(RTR Collection)*

London School of Flying instructors photographed in front of one of the school's DHC1 Chipmunks in 1959. From left to right; chief flying instructor John Schooling, Dick Blakeway, Scott Crawford, David Greenland, Mike Buxton, Ray Foote and Andy Pankhurst. *(The Aeroplane)*

The London School of Flying's Piper PA-30 Twin Comanche 160 G-ATEN, formerly N7483Y in America, flying from Elstree on 21 September 1965. *(RTR)*

Though nose-wheel aircraft were generally pooh-poohed by the London School of Flying one such example was briefly painted in the school's light/dark blue colour scheme. The first 150 to appear on the British register, 1957 Piper PA-22 Tri-Pacer G-APTP, is seen here at Elstree in the 1970s. *(RTR)*

The London School of Flying's Piper PA-23 Apache 160 G-ARMI, registered in 1961, flying locally on 12 March 1965 with CFI David Greenland piloting the aircraft from the right-hand seat. This Apache was used by the school for twin-engine instrument flying training at £24 per hour. *(RTR)*

This photograph was taken for the London School of Flying to show the recently built pilot training centre seen at right. Built at a cost of £20,000 the building housed student accommodation, classrooms, demonstration laboratories and offices under one roof. The School's fleet of ageing DHC1 Chipmunks, soon to be replaced by Piper Cherokees, is lined up while the School's Piper Apache G-ARMI hurries to get included in the picture. *(RTR)*

During 1964 the London School of Flying began equipping with Piper PA-28 Cherokee 140s and within a very short time the fleet consisted entirely of tricycle-undercarriage aircraft. Cherokee G-ATTJ, delivered in early 1966, is pictured landing at Elstree one summer's afternoon a year or two later. By early 1967 ten Cherokees equipped the school's fleet. *(RTR)*

London School of Flying's Piper PA-30 Twin Comanche 160 G-ATYF landing at Elstree in the 1960s. *(RTR)*

London School of Flying Piper PA-28 Cherokee 140 G-ATOK flying circuits and bumps at Elstree in 1967. *(RTR)*

Grumman-American AA-1B Trainer G-BDNW, imported into Britain in 1975, was operated by the London School of Flying on behalf of Mission Control Music. *(RTR)*

8 For Business and Pleasure

Being situated only 12 miles from London's Marble Arch, Elstree Aerodrome has always attracted smaller business aircraft as well as private individuals visiting the capital. A representative selection of visiting private and business aircraft follows.

During the early 1960s Elstree skies frequently vibrated to the scream of twin 360/380hp Lycoming engines as a clutch of Italian-built Piaggio P.166s regularly used Elstree to drop off/pick up VIP executives for business in London. G-APYP is pictured touching down at Elstree in about 1960. In January 1964 this 166 became VH-MMP and was still flying in 2003. *(RTR)*

DH80A Puss Moth G-ABDF, built in 1930, survived the war in storage and was restored to the civil register in 1948. Pictured at Elstree that same year G-ABDF crashed at Dunmow, Essex in May 1955. *(EJR)*

De Havilland DH86A G-ADVJ was first registered in 1936 and following a brief spell with Blackpool & West Coast Air Services Lt passed to Aer Lingus and became EI-ABK, named *Eire*. After the war the DH86 was restored to the British register and acquired by Bond Air Services and based at Gatwick. It was sold to Gulf Aviation Ltd in July 1951 and based in Bahrain, where it lapsed into disrepair and became derelict within a year. G-ADVJ is here pictured at Elstree in about 1947. *(EJR)*

Built in 1938 by the Tipsy Aircraft Company Ltd at Hanworth, Tipsy Trainer I G-AFKP was owned by F. Ellam and based at Thame when it visited Elstree in about 1947. It was sent out to Khartoum, Egypt by a subsequent owner in 1950 and crashed at Gedaref in the Sudan in June 1952. Note Elstree's early postwar wooden control tower in the background. *(EJR)*

DH94 Moth Minor G-AFOZ, built in 1939 at Hatfield, was first owned by the Redhill Flying Club. Surviving RAF impressment during the war 'OZ was restored to the register and operated by the RAF Flying Club and based at nearby Panshanger – note the Club badge forward of the front cockpit – and was photographed at Elstree in 1948. On 3 May 1975 G-AFOZ was written off following a crash during an air display at Turnhouse. *(EJR)*

Seen about to leave Elstree is the sole British-registered example of the Hirtenburg HS9A. G-AGAK was built at Hirtenburg, Austria in 1936 for J.H. Davis and registered OE-DJH. After a brief period as D-EDJH the aircraft was registered in Britain in 1939, still in Davis' name. This *rara avis* survived the war in storage at Filton, Bristol and passed through several postwar ownerships until acquired by Chris H. Cosmelli who based it at Denham. The owner crashed the Hirtenberg on Butser Hill, near Petersfield, Hampshire on 15 February 1958. *(RTR Collection)*

Built in 1941 Lockheed Model 12A G-AGTL was first registered in Britain in 1946 and is seen here at Elstree in 1959. At this time it was owned by K. McAlpine. Initially registered NC33615 this 12A later flew with the US Navy as 02947 and in 1939 was famously used by Sqn Ldr F.S. Cotton on radio development work for several years. Powered by two 450hp Pratt & Whitney Wasp Junior radial engines G-AGTL carried six passengers and two crew. It was sold in France as F-BJJY in 1960. *(RTR)*

Yellow Air Taxi Company's newly-acquired Auster Autocrat G-AHHL at Elstree in 1948. Based at Elmdon, Birmingham this charter company began operations in January 1948, continuing charters with a Proctor V, Percival Q6 and a Dragon Rapide until 1952. G-AHHL was written off in France on 27 September 1961. *(EJR)*

Miles M.65 Gemini 1A G-AHKL, built at Reading in 1946 and pictured at Elstree in 1948, was once owned by the Smithfield Refrigerator Company. It was withdrawn from use at Lympne, Kent in 1966. *(EJR)*

Percival Proctor 1 G-AHMR, built for the RAF as P6273 by Hills & Son of Manchester, at Elstree in 1947. It was lost in a crash at nearby South Mimms in May 1951 – see page 156. *(EJR)*

A couple of hours after this photograph was taken at Elstree on 7 July 1959 this DH89A Dragon Rapide crashed and burnt out on the M1 motorway spur to St Albans under construction at nearby Leverstock Green. Flown by W.A. 'Tubby' Ashton the aircraft was on charter to Tarmac, the motorway's main contractor, to take a party of visitors to view progress. The Rapide landed 700 yards from the end of the available strip but halfway down swung off to port. The pilot decided to overshoot but in doing so hit a car and a lorry and the Rapide crashed and caught fire. One passenger was fatally injured, two other passengers were seriously injured and a fourth was only slightly hurt. The pilot, half-hidden behind the Rapide in this picture, somehow managed to escape relatively unscathed through the tiny triangular cockpit window. He tried to repeat the exercise in another Rapide and found it impossible! *(RTR)*

Fox's Glacier Mints' D.H.89A Dragon Rapide G-AIDL was a regular caller at Elstree during the late 1950s and early 1960s. Built in 1946 this Rapide is now owned by Air Atlantique and gives pleasure flights at air displays. *(RTR)*

Members of the Herts & Essex Aero Club initially based at nearby Broxbourne frequently called in to Elstree during the 1940s and early 1950s. Seen here in about 1949 is G-AIDR, one of the club's Tiger Moths, doped silver overall with a green tail plume and sporting a blind-flying hood over the rear cockpit. In 1954 this Tiger was sold in New Zealand and became ZK-BEF. *(EJR)*

Beech 35 G-AJVG, with distinctive 'butterfly' tail, stands next to Elstree's Auster Autocrat G-AGXT in 1948. The Riding family's green Ford car can be seen parked by the hangar door. The following year the Bonanza was acquired by the Israeli Air Force and in 1956 became 4X-AER in that country before being sold as F-BCAQ in 1958. *(EJR)*

The short-lived four-seat KZ-VII Lark, registered G-AJZV in September 1947, and pictured at Elstree later that year. The Lark was powered by a 125hp Continental C-125-2 engine and on the side of the engine cowling is inscribed, 'R.K. Dundas Limited, sole UK agents'. This company imported a couple of Larks into Britain in 1947. On December 20 that year the Lark crashed near Manston, Kent. *(EJR)*

Fairchild Argus II G-AKJM at Elstree, seen here in about 1949, was sold in Australia in 1951 and became VH-AVN. *(RTR Collection)*

Chrislea C.H.3 Super Ace G-AKVF during a visit to Elstree from Barton for a Certificate of Airworthiness renewal by Simpsons Aeroservices in May 1962. The unusual controls were the cause of great consternation to Tim Davies, who carried out the Certificate of Airworthiness test flight. Instead of the control wheel being pulled and pushed for climb and descent it was moved vertically down and up. This unnatural arrangement was difficult enough to cope with in normal straight and level flight but when a sudden manoeuvre was required the pilot reverted to his natural instinct only to find the controls appeared to have locked! For this characteristic the aircraft earned for itself the sobriquet 'Grizzle Ace'! The pilot's comments in the remarks column of his log book make interesting reading! *(RTR)*

Piper L-4H Cub G-ALGH, previously 44-80545, is pictured at Elstree in about 1948 – it was sold in Iceland as TF-KAP in 1952. *(EJR)*

Pictured at Elstree in about 1959 is Avro 652A Anson Mk II G-AMBE, built in 1942 and formerly EG228 with the RAF. Often recorded as 'not converted, withdrawn from use' here is positive proof that the aircraft operated as G-AMBE. At the time of this photograph it was registered to Southend-based B.K.S. Engineering and operated by the Federated Fruit Company. *(RTR)*

This photograph of Tom Hayhow in his Auster Aiglet G-AMOS was taken on Good Friday 1952 in the vicinity of Elstree from an accompanying Miles Gemini flown by Nat Somers, at the conclusion of a record non-stop dash from Elstree–Paris–Toussus-le-Noble–Elstree. Note the non-standard tailskid. *(The Aeroplane)*

During 1952 and 1953 Tom Hayhow used Elstree, among other airfields, as a departure point on a series of Class C (1,102-2,204lb) record-breaking flights to and from Europe, all flown in his yellow and blue Auster J.5F Aiglet G-AMOS, named *Liege Lady*. Eighteen records, all flown from Elstree, were accomplished in one Easter weekend alone! One afternoon flight nearly ran into disaster. Returning to Elstree from Luxembourg Hayhow ran into heavy haze in the Thames Estuary. On reaching Mill Hill in north London the main tank emptied and, because it took some time for the fuel to flow from the wing tanks, the engine stopped and Hayhow hastily prepared to make a forced landing on Mill Hill golf course. Fortunately the engine caught in time and he was able to complete yet another record flight: Elstree–Luxembourg–Elstree in 4hr 55mins at an average speed of 129.5mph.

For the record flights the Auster was fitted with Decca Navigator and an additional fuel tank. These and subsequent record flights included: London to the Hague at 141mph on 11 April 1952, Brussels to London at 122mph on 12 April 1952, London to Copenhagen at 118mph on 30 May 1952, London–Berne–London at 141mph on 7 June 1952, Stockholm to London at 134.5mph on 9 August 1952 and Madrid to London at 115mph on 17 August 1952.

On 10 April 1953 Hayhow departed Elstree to have a crack at the London to Belgrade point-to-point record. He went missing and was eventually found to have perished from exposure after crashing in the Austrian Alps some 20 miles south-west of Salzburg.

Morton Air Services 1947 D.H. 104 Dove 1B G-AMYO taxiing in to drop off passengers at Elstree, c. 1959. Originally sold abroad as VP-YEV this Dove took up British marks in 1953. After service with Croydon-based Morton Air Services it was sold in Senegal in 1969. *(RTR)*

Thruxton Jackaroo G-ANFY began life as Tiger Moth NL906 with the RAF. In 1958 'FY became one of nineteen Tigers to be converted into a four-seat Thruxton Jackaroo. When it visited Elstree in 1959 the Jackaroo was owned by the Wiltshire School of Flying at Thruxton. G-ANFY was withdrawn from use in 1968 but has since been rebuilt. *(RTR)*

Miles M.14A Hawk Trainer G-ANWO, formerly L8262 with the RAF, was the last 'Maggie' to appear on the British civil register and was rebuilt by members of the Derby Airways Flying Group at Burnaston, Derby. Pictured at Elstree in 1959 G-ANWO was damaged in April 1962 and was preserved for a while by the Newark Air Museum. *(RTR)*

The arrival of this apparition caused much excitement in 1959. Scottish Aviation Twin Pioneer G-AOER operated by the Rio-Tinto Finance & Exploration Ltd was like no other 'Twin Pin'. The bits on the ends of the wings are not stabilisers but containers for airborne magnetometer equipment fitted for survey work in Mexico and California. In 1962 it was registered in Mexico as XC-CUJ and in 1964 it was sold to Tucson-based Arizona Airmotive. *(RTR)*

Visiting DH114 Herons were a rarity at Elstree. Morton Air Services Croydon-based G-AOXL was a Mk 1B built in 1953 and originally registered PH-GHB, taking up British registry in 1957. In 1972 the Heron was sold in Norway to become LN-BFY. *(RTR)*

The arrival at Elstree of this 58ft-span beast one day in 1959 caused quite a stir. Canadian-built DHC3 Otter G-AOYX was registered in May 1957 and was used for demonstration and communications work by de Havilland Aircraft. The Otter carried 14 passengers and two crew and was powered by a 600hp Pratt & Whitney Wasp, the sound of which could be heard for miles around when it took off from Elstree after its brief visit. In July 1961 G-AOYX, one of only two registered in Britain, was sold in Portugal. *(RTR)*

With its headquarters at nearby Stanmore the Automobile Association's (AA) aircraft were regular visitors to Elstree, particularly during the construction of the M1 motorway. Seen here at Elstree are the AA's Auster J.5R Alpine G-APAA and D.H. 89A Dragon Rapide G-AHKV, both doped in the AA's attractive yellow and black livery. The AA acquired the Alpine in 1956 and used it for two years; the subsequent owner retained the AA paint scheme for a period. The Rapide, previously owned by brewers Ind, Coope & Allsopp, remained in service with the AA during the 1950s and early 1960s and was finally withdrawn from use at Elmdon, Birmingham in 1969. *(RTR)*

Edgar Percival E.P.9 G-AOZO called in to Elstree from its birthplace at Stapleford on 23 December 1959 during a sales demonstration tour in the hands of the Earl of Bective. Richard Riding, with others, was given a ride and during a demonstration of the E.P.9's slow-flying abilities the aircraft practically hovered for a full minute. On 2 July 1980 G-AOZO crashed shortly after taking off from Lympne, Kent and burnt out. It was carrying parachutists and all six aboard lost their lives. *(RTR)*

Wg Cdr O.V. 'Titch' Holmes, whose company Airborne Taxi Services had operated from Elstree between 1946 and 1952, flew this blue Tiger Club Druine D.31 Turbulent G-APBZ into Elstree on 19 September 1958. 'BZ was damaged beyond repair in April 1963. This was the first aeroplane photograph to be taken by Richard Riding. *(RTR)*

With the lifting of UK import restrictions around 1958, American-built singles and twins began to flood the British light aircraft movement. The first Piper PA-23 Apache 150 to take up British registry was G-APCL, registered to the Earl of Derby and seen at Elstree in 1959. Re-registered in Ireland as EI-ANI in 1963-4 the Apache returned to British registry and was finally lost in a crash-landing at Shoreham in July 1972. *(RTR)*

C. Nepean Bishop was probably one of the best exponents of the Tiger Moth and the Miles Magister. For many years he was the Tiger Club's CFI and in his honour a special lightweight single seat Tiger Moth was converted by Rollasons at Croydon. Named *The Bishop* and registered G-APDZ its namesake performed aerobatic displays all over the country in company with similarly modified Tigers bearing clerical titles. *The Bishop*, pictured here at Elstree in 1959, was written off following a crash at Little Snoring in May 1960. *(RTR)*

Pictured outside Derby Aviation's workshop at Elstree in 1958 is the Druine D.5 Turbi G-APFA built by Britten-Norman Ltd and first flown in May 1957 by Desmond Norman from Bembridge on the Isle of Wight. In 1958 Elstree-based Ulair Ltd swapped the 65hp Coventry Victor Flying Neptune engine for a Continental engine of the same power and added a glazed canopy. Though the aircraft's Permit to Fly expired in 1992 the aircraft was still registered in 2003. *(RTR Collection)*

BKS Survey's Avro 19 Series 2 G-APHV taxis out from Elstree in about 1962 to return to Southend. Formerly VM360 with the RAF this Anson was first registered in 1958 to Hants and Sussex Aviation Ltd. It was later based in Ireland with Survey Flights Ltd befor being acquired, with many of its brethren, by Thruxton-based Kemps Aerial Surveys. *(RTR)*

Percival Prentice I G-APIY *Oracle II*, previously VR249 with the RAF, took up British registry in July 1958. Named *The Keri Lyn* it was based at Rhoose, Cardiff. It passed through several more ownerships before being acquired by the Laarbruch Flying Club in 1965 and based in Germany. G-APIY was withdrawn from use in 1967 but is currently with the Newark Air Museum. *(RTR)*

D.H. 89A Dragon Rapide 4 G-APJW, registered in May 1958, was built just up the road at Hatfield as X7437. Powered by a pair of DH Gipsy Queen 2 engines the Rapide was owned by Direct Air Ltd. It was a regular visitor to Elstree before being sold abroad in 1962 to become F-BHOB. *(RTR)*

Crop Culture's scruffy workhorse Auster J.1N Alpha G-APKL about to leave Elstree in 1959 to return to its Bembridge, Isle of Wight base. Used for crop spraying this Alpha is fitted with Britten-Norman rotary atomisers below the wingtips and on both sides of the fuselage. Sold to Portsmouth Aero Club shortly after this photograph was taken, G-APKL was lost in July 1963 when it crashed on the beach near Le Touquet, France. *(RTR)*

The flood of Piper Apaches from Lock Haven, USA to the UK began with a trickle in 1957. Piper PA-23 Apache 160 G-APLJ was the second 160 to be registered in Britain, in June 1958, and is seen at Elstree the following year. After being sold to Nigeria in 1960 as VR-NDG this aircraft was sold in Australia as VH-DRR in 1963. *(RTR)*

G-APUZ, the first Piper PA-24 Comanche 250 registered in Britain, in July 1959, is seen at Elstree in 1960. Built at Lock Haven, USA the blue and white four-seater was powered by a 250hp Lycoming O-540-A1D5 engine. Its smooth lines, retractable undercarriage and 180mph cruising speed caused a great deal of interest with CPL students learning to cope with the idiosyncrasies of the Auster Autocrat! More than forty years later this Comanche was still airworthy and registered to Tatenhill Aviation Ltd. *(RTR)*

Built in 1959 Piaggio P.166 G-APWY was registered in January 1961 and based at nearby Luton. Powered by two 340hp 'pusher' Lycoming GSO-480-B1C6 engines mounted in the gull-wings, the elegant P.166 cruised at around 210mph. G-APWY was initially operated by Marconi as a flying laboratory and was a regular visitor to Elstree, much to the annoyance of the neighbours! At the time of writing the aircraft was owned by the Science Museum. *(RTR)*

Francis Freeman and the late Charles Crichton-Stuart about to leave Elstree in the brand new silver and maroon Aeromere F.8L Falco Series III G-APXD in 1960. This immaculate 26ft 3in-span wooden two-seater was an essay in aerodynamic perfection. Designed by Italian Stelio Ftati the Falco was powered by a 160hp Lycoming O-320-B3B engine which gave a cruising speed of 180mph. *(RTR)*

Old Cessnas never die . . . G-APXY was the first of many hundreds of Cessna 150s imported into Britain from Wichita and later France and is seen at Elstree in 1960. The all-metal two-seater was first produced in 1958 and was initially powered by the 100hp Continental 0-200-A engine. Previously N7911E in America G-APXY was registered in Britain in March 1960 and more than forty years later was flying with the Merlin Flying Club Ltd. *(RTR)*

Orlikan Meta-Sokol L.40 G-ARJO pictured at Elstree on 23 May 1962. Note the reversed tricycle undercarriage of this four-seat tourer. Registered in the UK in April 1961 'JO crashed at Biggin Hill on 4 June 1965. *(RTR)*

G-ARKE, the prototype Beagle A.109 Airedale after it was fitted with a British-built 175hp Rolls-Royce Continental engine and larger spinner to become the sole A.111. When it visited Elstree in about 1961 the Airedale was covered in wool tufts, presumably to study airflow behaviour in the new configuration. *(RTR)*

These two photographs are included because they feature two almost identical aircraft photographed from the same spot on two completely different occasions. Above is Sir N. Nuttall's Helio H-395 Super Courier G-ARLD, built in 1961 and formerly N13B and N1890B in the USA, making a typical Stol take-off from Elstree c. 1962. Below is Super Courier G-ARMU, also built in 1961 and also formerly N13B, and later N4172D, making a similar departure from Elstree. For a while Strathallan Air Services owned this aircraft until it was sold in Ireland to become EI-ATG. After returning to the British register this Courier was lost in a crash at Ormesby Hall, Norfolk on 30 August 1970. *(RTR)*

Scottish Aviation Twin Pioneer G-ASHN, originally registered EP-AGB in 1957, was owned by Keegan Aviation when it dropped in to Elstree in 1963. Later that year the 'Twin Pin' was sold abroad and became HC-AHT. *(RTR)*

Tim Davies flying the beautifully proportioned Procaer F.15B Picchio 3 G-ARNV from Elstree on 27 September 1964. Registered in September 1961 this all-wood four-seater crashed near Ramsey, Isle of Man on 9 September 1969. *(RTR)*

Nord 1101 Noralpha G-ASTN, previously F-BLTR, was built in 1945 and the first British-registered example of its type. Pictured at Elstree in 1964 the aircraft was written off at Oldenburg in Germany in August the same year. *(RTR)*

The weird-looking Dornier Do 28A-1 Skyservant, with no visible means of support for its wing, was an all-metal six-passenger Stol aircraft powered by two 290hp Lycoming engines mounted on stub wings. Built in 1964 G-ASUR was one of two British-registered examples and was owned for many years by Sheffair Ltd and based at Tollerton. It was still airworthy at the time of writing. *(RTR)*

A nice view of Orlikan Super Aero 45 G-ASYY, built in 1955, landing at Elstree one Sunday afternoon, c. 1961. The excellent view from the cockpit is very apparent in this view. *(RTR)*

For a brief period in the late 1960s the Australian-designed Vicata Airtourer 100 G-ATJC flew for a trial period with the London School of Flying. G-ATJC was still airworthy at the time of writing. *(RTR)*

A precursor of things to come. During early 1971 nearby Leavesden Aerodrome became the distribution point for the American Aviation AA-1 Yankee, handled by General Aviation Sales of Jersey. Richard Riding was asked to take some publicity photographs of a batch of four aircraft: G-AYLM –' LP. For this purpose Dave Blackburn flew G-AYLO across to Elstree and threw it around the sky in far from ideal winter conditions. Within a short space of time the two-seat AA-1 and the four-seat AA-5 Traveler were equipping many clubs and schools up and down the country. G-AYLO was damaged beyond economic repair in September 1984. *(RTR)*

On 19 September 1976 six former Spanish Air Force CASA 1.131E Jungmanns descended upon Elstree having been ferried in formation from Spain by owner Spencer Flack and members of the 'Elstree Air Force'. G-BEDA, pictured here shortly after its arrival at Elstree, was acquired by Personal Plane Services at Booker and, together with two others from the original batch of nine, is still airworthy at the time of writing. *(RTR)*

Cessna 340 G-BBAA, built in 1973 and previously N7852Q, pictured at Elstree in 1974. G-BBAA was sold in Sweden in November 1975 and became SE-GOC. *(RTR)*

9 Rotary Club

Some of Elstree's rotary-winged residents and visitors.

Left a bit! Ace chopper pilot Frank Laycock, right, plops Bell 47G G-AVSK onto a trailer with inches to spare at the back of Elstree's main hangar, c. 1971. G-AVSK was written off when it spun into trees from 20ft on Valentine's Day 1973 while top dressing in Glentrool Forest, Wigtown. (RTR)

This curious looking little contraption caused a great deal of interest at Elstree in May 1958 during a sales tour of Britain and Europe. After an assembly time of three minutes the Hiller XROE-1 Rotorcycle N6728C was demonstrated on the lawn in front of the flying club. A conventional helicopter in miniature the Rotorcycle was powered by a 45hp Nelson two-stroke piston engine, cruised at 55mph and had a top speed of 70mph. The machine's unladen weight was 350lb, fully loaded 556lb and the range, including 180-lb pilot and 60lb pack, was 34 miles. *(RTR Collection)*

British European Airways (BEA) Westland Sikorsky S-55 Whirlwind Series 1 G-ANFH at Elstree in about 1960. First flown in 1954 it was owned by BEA from 1954 until it passed to BEA Helicopters Ltd in 1964. It was sold to Bristow Helicopters in 1969 and is currently preserved at the Helicopter Museum in Weston-super-Mare. *(RTR)*

This Westland Sikorsky S-51 Series 2 Widgeon G-ANLW began life as a Mk 1A in 1954 but was converted to a Widgeon in 1958, the year this photograph was taken at Elstree. It is currently preserved at the Norfolk & Suffolk Aviation Museum near Bungay. *(RTR)*

Westland-Sikorsky S-51 Mk 1A G-ANZL was originally registered G-ANAL but was re-registered in March 1955 to the Fairey Aviation Company Ltd. G-ANZL was written off near Netheravon, Wiltshire, in October 1959 shortly after this photograph was taken during a visit to Elstree. *(RTR)*

Westland Sikorsky S-51 Widgeon G-APPR, in the livery of British United Airways, taking off from Elstree. *c.* 1960. In June 1962 the S.51 went out to Nigeria as 5N-ABV. *(RTR)*

BEA Agusta-Bell 47J G-APTH at Elstree, *c.* 1960. Sold abroad as 5N-ACP in 1963 'TH is currently stored. *(RTR)*

During the building of the M1 motorway in 1958 John Laing engineers and VIPs were flown to view work in progress in Executair's Westland S-51 Widgeon G-APTW, leased by Westland Aircraft Ltd and flown by Captain Bird. The London School of Flying's Avro 19 G-AGWE can be seen in the background. G-APTW is currently preserved at the Newark Air Museum. *(RTR)*

Benson B-7M Gyroplane G-APUD was built by Wg Cdr Ken Wallis and first flown in June 1959. Not long afterwards it was flown over to Elstree following a demonstration at nearby Bentley Priory and very nearly landed in Hilfield Reservoir adjoining the aerodrome. *(Brian Turpin)*

John Crewdson departs from Elstree in the Westland Widgeon G-APWK; note the camera rig. G-APWK was withdrawn from use in 1970. *(RTR)*

This Redhill-based Hiller UH-12E G-ATVG of the Central Electricity Generating Board was a frequent visitor to Elstree engaged upon its task of pylon inspection – Elstree's notorious pylons converge on a grid station less than a mile west of the main runway. Resuming its travels after a tea break the Hiller takes off over London School of Flying Chipmunk G-AOSY and Cherokee G-ATTJ. G-ATVG was sold in 1967 and became EP-HAL. *(RTR)*

Sud-Aviation 318C Alouette II G-AWEE of Samuelson Aviation Ltd was based at Elstree from early 1969 and is seen here being flown by Capt John Crewdson in about 1970. Crewdson was killed in this helicopter in a collision with SE5A replica EI-ARB/G-ATGW during filming off Wicklow Head on 18 August 1970. *(RTR)*

Sud-Aviation 341G Gazelle 2 G-BAGL, powered by one Turbomeca Astazou IIIA, was registered in October 1972 and was initially operated by Westland Helicopters Ltd and latterly by Triangle Computer Services Ltd. *(David Oliver)*

10 Elstree Miscellany

A selection of gliders, amphibians, overseas-registered and service types that have resided at or visited Elstree since the war.

Pilot's-eye view during final approach to Elstree, photographed from Piper J3C Cub HB-OCH flown by John Greenland during the summer of 1978. *(RTR)*

On 1 April 1949 the Ministry of Civil Aviation decreed that all gliders should be given Class A marks, i.e. carry registration letters in the same way as powered aircraft. The first glider so registered was Chilton Olympia sailplane G-ALJN/BGA434. The glider registration scheme was short-lived and was discontinued in 1950 after about 145 gliders had been registered, mostly in the G-AL registration sequence. Owned by Dudley Hiscox G-ALJN was based at Elstree for a while and was sold in Ireland in 1961. Although the marks EI-103 were reserved they were not taken up and the glider was withdrawn from use in 1963. These two views were taken at Elstree in 1949. *(EJR)*

Eon Type 5 Olympia G-ALMY/BGA532 was owned by G.H. Stephenson and J.C. Dent when this photograph was taken at Elstree in about 1948. The glider was withdrawn from use in March 1963. *(EJR)*

Lake LA-4-180 Amphibian G-BASO, its British marks barely obscuring the American registration letters N2025L, was imported into Britain by Elstree-based Medburn Air Services Ltd. This photograph was taken shortly after the Lake arrived at Elstree in 1973. *(RTR)*

Another Medburn Air Services import was Lake LA-4-200 G-BBGK, pictured at Elstree, c. 1973. The amphibian was later re-registered G-PARK. *(RTR)*

Seen about to depart from Elstree in about 1966 is the Grumman G.21 Goose G-ASXG, formerly '926' with the Royal Canadian Air Force. Operated on behalf of Grosvenor Estates and based at Hawarden the Goose is seen here fitted with two 450hp Pratt & Whitney Wasp Junior engines. The aircraft was later re-engined with 550hp Pratt & Whitney PT-6A-20 propeller turbines. Note the floats retracted into the wingtips. The aircraft returned to Canada in 1973 and became CF-AWH. *(RTR)*

D-FGAL, a skywriting North American AT-6A Texan, dropped into Elstree in about 1959 and it may have been the Texan that wrote 'Super Mac' in the skies above Southend ahead of that year's General Election, held on 8 October. First registered in Germany as D-IGAL to Deutscher Luftfahrt Beratungsdienst, Wiesbaden the Texan is currently (2003) stored at Hilversum, Holland. *(RTR)*

There was nothing mundane about this Cessna 182 pictured at Elstree in April 1971. Formerly N2096X in America this 182's wing has been modified for slow-speed flying and the aircraft was redesignated Cessna 182/Wren 460. It was initially owned by the Irish Parachute Club and was based for a while at Edenderry. *(RTR)*

Ranger-engined Fairchild 24R F-BENN at Elstree, c. 1948. Built as a UC-61K Forwarder and flown as HB757 by the RAF during the war this four-seat communications aircraft was sold to R.S. McCall as F-BENN in 1948. *(EJR)*

Druine Turbulent F-PHFR was flown over to Elstree from Paris by Harold Best-Devereux on the afternoon of 8 April 1956 and loitered a while before returning to France. During its stay at Elstree many local pilots sampled the delights of flying this Arden-powered ultralight. In this photograph Best-Devereux is seen on the Elstree taxiway prior to setting off on another demonstration flight. At the time of writing this veteran Turbulent was still around and was offered for sale at around £6,000. *(RTR Collection)*

Douglas DC-3 N47FL parked at Elstree in October 1995, with DC-3 N47FK/EC-FNS behind. N47FL suffered damage to one of its wings on 17 July 1996 when American Aviation AA-5A Cheetah G-FANG slewed off the runway when landing and ran into the Dakota. Though the DC-3 was lightly damaged the Cheetah was damaged beyond economical repair. *(GRP)*

NC6430N was one of several Piper L-4 Cubs operated by the American Embassy Flying Club during the late 1940s and early 1950s. Pictured here at Elstree in about 1950 this Cub was registered G-AKNC until sold to the Embassy in mid-1948. *(Arthur W.J.G. Ord-Hume)*

Ted Smith Aerostar 601 N7480S called in to Elstree in November 1970. It was written off at Fort Worth, Texas, in July the following year. *(RTR)*

Zlin 226 Trener OK-KMA pictured at Elstree with several of its Czech mates during a mass visit to Elstree, c. 1962. *(RTR)*

Opposite: The Bjorn Andreasson BA-4B single-seat aerobatic biplane SE-XBS at Elstree in 1968 where, for obvious reasons, it was known by the sobriquet 'Sexy Beast'! Powered by a 100hp Continental 0-200-A engine the 17ft 6in-span machine was later registered G-AWPZ in November 1968 and demonstrated up and down the country by the late Peter Phillips, who had acquired the design and production rights from designer Bjorn Andreasson. *(RTR)*

Orlikan Morava L-200A OK-PLD was one of several Czechoslovakian types that turned up at Elstree one day, c. 1962. This development of the Aero 145 was powered by two 210hp Letadlovy M-337 engines and first appeared in 1960. *(RTR)*

Cessna Citation 1/SP 501 VP-CAT at Elstree on 22 August 1997. Earlier, on 2 July, this aircraft was slightly damaged following loss of control after touching down on Runway 26. Damage was restricted to the tail cone, slight scraping to the underside and a damaged starboard wheel – no one was hurt. *(GRP)*

DH89B Dominie I NF867, built by Brush Coachworks at Loughborough in 1944 and delivered to the Royal Navy, is seen during a brief visit to Elstree one winter's day in 1959. *(RTR)*

Percival Proctor 3 G-AGWB was formerly flying with the RAF as LZ734. It was issued with a Certificate of Airworthiness in May 1946 but was returned to the RAF and reverted to its old RAF serial number in November 1951. It was de-mobbed once again and restored to the register in March 1957. For a while the Proctor was flown in its old RAF livery and as such is seen at Elstree in the early 1960s. In August 1967 the aircraft was damaged beyond repair at Moulton near Darlington. *(RTR)*

DHC1 Chipmunk T.10 WK577, powered by a DH Gipsy Major 10 Mk 2 engine and built for the RAF in 1950, is pictured during a visit to Elstree in May 1970. In March 1975 the Chipmunk was registered as G-BCYM and is currently airworthy. *(RTR)*

Hunting Percival Provost T.1 XF900, built during 1955/6, was originally attached to the Royal Air Force College, Cranwell. At the time of its visit to Elstree in about 1962, it was on the strength of the Central Flying School. This Provost was taken off RAF charge in November 1963. *(RTR)*

DHC2 Beaver XP807 was delivered to the Army Air Corps in 1961 and is pictured here about to leave Elstree in the late 1960s. The Beaver was written off on 14 May 1971. *(RTR)*

Army Air Corps Auster AOP. 9 XK406, built at Rearsby in 1956, pictured on arrival at Elstree in the 1960s. *(RTR)*

Bristol 171 Sycamore HR. 14 XG502 was delivered to the RAF in August 1955 and was written off on 1 January 1964. Seen here at Elstree in about 1962, XG502 is currently on static exhibition at the Museum of Army Flying at Middle Wallop in Hampshire. *(RTR)*

Westland Sioux A.H. 1. XT563 of the Army Air Corps pictured at Elstree in the late 1970s. XT563 was broken up at Southend in 1981. *(RTR)*

11 Down in the Dumps

On every aerodrome there is some corner where aircraft damaged beyond repair are consigned to the mercy of the elements. Elstree is no exception and the following photographs afford a final glimpse of aircraft that have passed their sell-by date.

This photograph, taken in September 1947, shows Elstree's first postwar dump, located at the rear of the main hangar. In the foreground are the skeletal remains of the DH82A Tiger moth G-AJHN – see page 166. In the background can be seen the hulk of the LAMS Halifax G-AHZM – see page 45. *(Arthur W.J.G. Ord-Hume)*

Comper Swift G-ABPE survived the war and was purchased by Adrian B. Golay but written off by him on 26 April 1947 while taking off from a field near St Albans. While some of the Swift's parts were used by Tony Cole in the rebuilding of Swift G-ABUS, the wings, undercarriage and nose section were acquired by Arthur W.J.G. Ord-Hume and taken to Elstree in November 1948, when this photograph was taken. These relics were later stored by E.J. Riding at his home in Hendon and after his death in April 1950 the remains remained at Hendon until disposed of in the 1960s. *(Arthur W.J.G. Ord-Hume)*

On 30 May 1951 Percival Proctor I G-AHMR crashed at South Mimms and for many weeks its remains languished between Hangars 2 and 3 at Elstree, where this photograph was taken on 29 June 1951. *(Arthur W.J.G. Ord-Hume)*

Miles M.14A Hawk Trainer G-AHYL gave sterling service to the flying school at Elstree throughout the 1950s until the 'Maggie' fleet became redundant in 1959. CFI W.H. 'Bill' Bailey flew 'YL in the 1957 King's Cup air race. In private hands G-AHYL was painted in a waspish yellow and black colour scheme. In 1960 an exuberant pilot flew through, rather than over, a five-bar gate and lost an undercarriage leg. The aircraft was damaged beyond repair in the subsequent landing and languished, disgraced, behind the main hangar until burnt. *(RTR)*

A 'hangar queen' at Elstree for many years was Miles M. 57 Aerovan G-AMYC, one of two uncompleted aircraft built by Handley Page (Reading) Ltd and sold to Air Ads Ltd in the early 1950s. Aerovan G-AMYA was moved from Elstree to Croydon in 1955 and subsequently scrapped while G-AMYC remained gathering dust and much more in the main hangar at Elstree. This photograph was taken in about 1959, when the cream and red-trimmed Aerovan was hauled out and taken by road to Stapleford. Earmarked for preservation this historic aircraft probably provided the centre-piece for a November 5th celebration at a later date! *(RTR)*

Airspeed A.S. 65 Consul G-AJXE, formerly HN734 in the RAF, received its first Certificate of Airworthiness in September 1947. Its last flight was made on the day it arrived at Elstree in 1959. The Consul remained behind the main hangar gradually deteriorating until it was eventually burnt. *(RTR)*

De Havilland DH82A Tiger Moth G-APIP pictured behind the main hangar at Elstree, c. 1959. Owned by Vendair (London) Ltd of Croydon and formerly T5843 in the RAF this Tiger received its first Certificate of Airworthiness in July 1958. It may have escaped from being dumped as the records note that G-APIP crashed at Hayes Common, Kent in July 1963. *(RTR)*

12 Prangs

Although busier than most small aerodromes Elstree mercifully has witnessed few fatal accidents in its seventy-year history.

London School of Flying DHC1 Chipmunk G-APTG pictured on 3 October 1965 after it was written off at the western end of Elstree's runway. The culprit crawled out without a scratch and, like a Victorian big game hunter with his kill, is pictured posing with the badly wrecked aircraft. *(RTR)*

Slingsby T.7 Cadet T.2 VM685 overturned at Elstree, c. 1947. Here it is surrounded by ATC cadets, presumably from No. 124 ATC Gliding School. The damage to the glider was only minimal and restricted mostly to the crushed fin and rudder and no doubt it was back in the air in no time. *(EJR)*

This photograph of Miles M. 38 Messenger G-ALBR taken after it crashed into trees near the Battle Axes Inn at the eastern end of Elstree's runway after taking off on 2 July 1949. Formerly RH378 with the RAF this Messenger was issued with its first Certificate of Airworthiness in September 1948 and was owned for a while by the record-breaking pilot Tom Hayhow. *(Arthur W.J.G. Ord-Hume)*

On 15 September 1947 Phyllis Mairet and Ralph Edwards were preparing for a flight in DH82A Tiger Moth G-AJHN, operated by LAMS, when it caught fire during starting. Though the pilot escaped without injury the lady, who was sitting in the cockpit at the time, suffered from burns and severe shock. *(EJR)*

Formerly on the strength of Derby Aviation's Elstree-based 'Maggie' fleet Miles M.14A Hawk Trainer G-AKKR returned to Elstree and flew with the Roy Mills' group of aircraft that included the Currie Wot G-APWT (see page 85) and the Fairchild Argus G-AIZE (see pages 172 and 173). G-AKKR had a habit of shedding undercarriage legs and this photograph illustrates just one such occasion. The aircraft was later painted in an all-black scheme and one day hit the jackpot and shed both legs simultaneously! Despite this G-AKKR has outlived its many hundred brethren and today is preserved for posterity and exhibited at the RAF Museum at Hendon painted as an RAF trainer. *(RTR)*

The London School of Flying's Chipmunks put in many thousands of hours giving hundreds of PPL and CPL students their wings. Every so often they would end up in local fields, mostly as a result of practice forced landing approaches that ended rather too realistically – carburettor icing generally being the culprit. In nearly all cases the aircraft were either flown out or retrieved by road and returned to the air fairly quickly. The two incidents recorded here took place in the early 1960s. G-APTG is seen in a field of barley on farmland just outside the Elstree circuit. The barley was too long for the student to fly out and an instructor carried out the tricky take-off with minimum damage to the crop. *(RTR)*

London School of Flying DHC1 Chipmunk G-APOE pictured shortly after it overturned during a forced landing into a ploughed field in the early 1960s. Damage was only superficial but the aircraft had to be dismantled and returned to Elstree by road. *(RTR)*

B.K.S. Engineering's Avro 652A Anson 11 G-ALXH pictured after its starboard undercarriage leg collapsed at Elstree while on lease to Huntings for photographic work, c. 1961. Built for the RAF as Anson 1 W1731 in 1940 G-ALXH was delivered to BKS in 1954. During 1955 the aircraft was rebuilt incorporating the fuselage of Anson PH808 and converted into a Mk 11. G-ALXH was written off at Guiseley, Yorkshire on 9 April 1963. *(RTR)*

This is another view of DHC1 Chipmunk G-APTG after its spectacular crash at Elstree on 3 October 1965. The unscathed pilot escaped via the cockpit canopy side panel but the aircraft was a total write-off. *(RTR)*

This page and opposite, top: All crashes are unpleasant but one of Elstree's worst, although it occurred just outside the boundary of the aerodrome, was the tragic accident to Saab Safir 91A G-ARFX. This former Dutch-registered Swedish-built aircraft took up British marks in 1960 and was registered to Welton Auto Services Ltd. On July 15, 1962 the owner turned up with two women employees to whom he had promised a flight. Despite the poor weather, the cloud base was about 300ft in rain; the pilot probably not wishing to disappoint his passengers took off and immediately entered the low cloud. Seconds later the Saab dived into the ground midway between the aerodrome and Elstree village a mile and a half away and burst into flames. All three occupants were killed instantly. *(RTR)*

This former French-registered Nord 1002 Pingouin had a very short life as a British registered aircraft. While taking off from Elstree on 30 July 1964 the aircraft ground-looped and lost an argument with the concrete fence that prevented it from ending up in the adjacent reservoir. *(RTR)*

Chronological listing of selected crashes at Elstree

19 September 1937 Hawker Demon K3802
This 601 (County of London) Squadron Demon flown by PO T.E. Hubbard was carrying out a practice forced landing approach at Elstree. On landing the undercarriage collapsed and the Demon turned on its nose.

1939 Aeronca 100
Brand-new aircraft being ferried from factory at Peterborough to base at Hanworth. The pilot, who was the son of Aircraft Exchange & Mart's Managing Director, decided to break the journey and stop for lunch at the Aldenham House Club. On his return to the aerodrome, he swung the propeller, presumably with the wheels chocked, and the aircraft rolled forward and became airborne. The pilot chased after the aircraft but was unable to catch it. Hit by a gust of wind the Aeronca nose-dived into a ditch after a wheel hit a fence and sustained a broken propeller and a bent undercarriage leg.

4 July 1942 Percival Proctor 1 P6320
This 171 Squadron aircraft, flown by PO H.J.P. Tyson, lost power during take-off, drifted into a tree and crashed.

8 July 1942 Boulton Paul Defiant II AA543
One of a formation of Defiants of the RAF Northolt Station Flight passing to the west of the aerodrome, this aircraft was seen to be trailing glycol. The pilot broke away and made an emergency downwind landing at Elstree but undershot hitting a line of tree stumps where trees had been felled to extend the runway. The pilot, PO D.C. Leonard was killed but his gunner escaped uninjured.

Between Autumn 1944 and April 1945 Consolidated B24 Liberator
This aircraft was flying en route from Bovingdon to Hendon in misty weather and attempted an emergency landing against the controller's instructions. On landing the B24 burst both mainwheel tyres, hit a small tree with its starboard wing tip and ran off the runway, coming to rest in a field adjacent to Aldenham Road. There were no casualties among the crew. The Army stood guard on the aircraft all night and next day a repair party arrived from Bovingdon. After repairs had been carried out the B24 was flown out the same day.

5 June 1944 Airspeed Oxford DF514
En route from Hethel to Bovingdon the pilot became lost and decided to land at Aldenham to seek directions. On landing he overshot the runway and stopped against the boundary hedge, sustaining only minor damage. Pilot Capt Hector J. Streyckmans of the US 8th Air Force admitted error of judgement.

16 September 1946 Handley Page C. Mk 8 Halifax G-AHZM
This London Aero & Motor Services freighter lost its port undercarriage during its Certificate of Airworthiness test flight. See photograph on page 45.

15 September 1947 De Havilland DH 82A Tiger Moth G-AJHN
Miss Phyllis Mary Mairet of North Mimms and Ralph Osborn Edwards were preparing for a flight. As soon as the propeller was swung the aircraft caught fire. See photograph on page 161.

2 July 1949 Miles M.38 Messenger 4A G-ALBR
Crashed almost immediately after taking off from Elstree bound for Deauville, France and came down in trees near Aldenham House. See photograph on page 160.

10 September 1952 Miles M.3A Falcon Major G-ADLI
While taking off from Elstree the aircraft hit a tree. The pilot and passengers were not badly hurt but the aircraft was written off.

8 November 1953 Miles M.14A Hawk Trainer G-AKRT
Registered to Wolverhampton Aviation: groundlooped and written off.

28 November 1954 Miles M.2F Hawk Major G-ACYO
Owned by Howard Stirling, it crashed on landing – cause not known. The aircraft was a total loss, and Howard's passenger was killed.

19 August 1956 Miles M.14A Hawk Trainer G-AJJI
Registered to Wolverhampton Aviation. Following a heavy landing the aircraft swung off the runway into corn and sustained heavy damage.

2 June 1957 Miles M.14A Hawk Trainer G-AHNW
Registered to Wolverhampton Aviation Ltd, it sustained serious damage while landing.

15 July 1962 Saab 91A Safir G-ARFX
The owner took off in appalling weather – low visibility and 300ft cloud base – and spun in seconds after entering cloud. See photographs on pages 164 and 165.

30 July 1964 Nord 1002 Pingouin G-ASUA
Ground-looped during take-off, hit the concrete fence bordering the aerodrome and the reservoir and was written off. See photograph on page 165.

3 October 1965 DHC1 Chipmunk G-APTG
Crashed on landing – no one injured but the aircraft was a write-off. See photographs on pages 159 and 163.

27 January 1968 Piper PA-23 Apache 150 G-ARHJ
Took off from Elstree for demonstration with potential buyer on board. The aircraft lost an engine and veered off to the left of the runway and crashed into the reservoir. All occupants were drowned. See photograph on page 89.

29 November 1975 Piper PA-23-250 Aztec D N6645Y
Elstree-based racing driver/owner Graham Hill was returning from Marseilles, France at night when he crashed on Arkley Golf Course in fog 3 miles out from Elstree while on final approach.

17 July 1996 Grumman AA-5A Cheetah G-FANG
The aircraft bounced on landing and yawed uncontrollably to port and hit and slightly damaged the underside of a parked DC-3. The student pilot escaped uninjured but the aircraft was damaged beyond economical repair.

13 People

Some of Elstree's 'characters' and a mix of 'celebrities'.

Montclare Shipping Company employees Oliver Williams, Tom Kilcoyne and 'Jock' Russell take a breather in front of Elstree's main hangar, c. 1970. Tom Kilcoyne kept a succession of John Houlder's aeroplanes airworthy over a period of more than twenty-five years (Miles Gemini G-ALCS, Cessna 310 G-ARBI and Aero Commander G-AWOE). 'Jock' Russell, ably assisted by a series of dogs named Haggis, was responsible for the day-to-day running of the aerodrome for several decades. The terror of aircraft spotters, he boasted that he ate them for breakfast. 'Jock' never seemed to age, retaining a full head of dark hair till his retirement. (RTR)

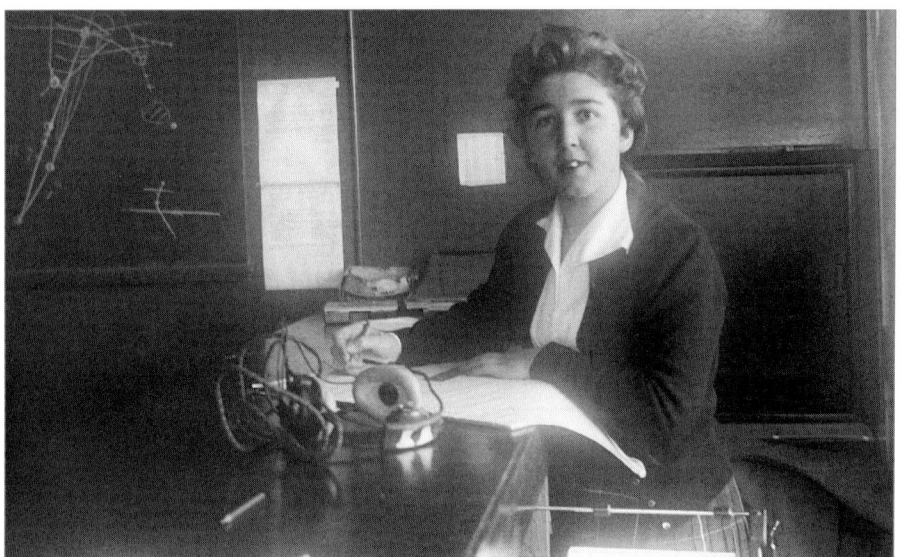

Elstree Flying Club Secretary Sheila Brunt pictured in her office, c. 1950. *(Arthur W.J.G. Ord-Hume)*

In addition to having a reputation for high standards of flying Elstree Flying Club has traditionally been very strong on social events like this club party, c. 1959. Top table: -?-, -?-, John and Eileen Houlder, Ron Paine, -?-, -?-, -?-, David Ogilvy, -?-, Peter Laffy. Diagonal table, from nearest camera, clockwise: Fred Marsh, Mr and Mrs Sid Aarons, Deidrie McCrae, -?-, -?-, -?-, -?- , Francis Newton, Eileen Riding, David Greenland, -?-, Table behind, with back to camera, Mike Buxton. *(RTR Collection)*

Another Elstree Flying Club party, c. 1960. At the top of the table can be seen C. Nepean Bishop, a former CFI at Elstree back in the 1940s, David Ogilvy and Mr Cox. *(RTR Collection)*

The clubhouse and bar at Elstree pictured c. 1962. The late Roger Healey and Dave Antrobus are in deep discussion at left. In mid-mouthful in the foreground is Derby Aerosurveys boss Col H.C. Butcher DSO and a group of CPL students can be seen chatting at right. *(RTR Collection)*

Left: London School of Flying instructor Miss Janet Ferguson taking a break between flights in 1960. One of Britain's greatest but unsung female pilots, Janet later spent more than thirty years ferrying aircraft to all parts of the world. *(RTR)*

Below: John Schooling, John 'Tubby' Simpson and Tony Samuelson discuss the performance of Spitfire Tr. 9 G-AVAV following an early dual flight in 1969. *(RTR)*

John 'Tubby' Simpson was one of Elstree's earliest characters and is seen here with Tony Samuelson's Hawker Hurricane G-AWLW in 1968. 'Tubby' worked for LAMS at Elstree in 1946 and remained on the aerodrome, running Simpsons Aeroservices, until his death in December 1969. A recognised expert on Rolls-Royce Merlin engines he was mainly responsible for keeping the aircraft flying for the epic *Battle of Britain* movie of 1968. *(RTR)*

William 'Bill' Bailey has spent nearly 50 years at Elstree, initially in an instructing capacity as CFI of the Elstree Flying Club and latterly as a Certificate of Airworthiness test pilot and St John Ambulance pilot. Except for John Houlder Bill has probably been associated with Elstree Aerodrome longer than anyone else. He is seen here shortly before making a Certificate of Airworthiness test flight in the WAR Focke-Wulf 190 scale replica G-WULF in January 1980. *(RTR)*

For many years Pete Woods was the voice of Elstree. He was the air traffic controller from the 1960s until his early death in a driving accident in about 1983. An aviation enthusiast through and through, his laid-back, almost laconic ATC patter belied Elstree's incredibly high air traffic volume during his occupancy of the tower. *(RTR)*

Between 1960 and 1964 BBC TV ran a series of around sixty editions of *It's a Square World,* devised by and starring the late Michael Bentine, supported by such actors as Clive Dunn and Frank Thornton. In one episode Bentine featured a no frills, but plenty of thrills, airline run on a shoestring and starring himself and Clive Dunn as the entire staff. This particular episode was filmed at Elstree in about 1963 and featured Roy Mills's Fairchild Argus G-AIZE. The sequence was shot in the 'frying pan' at the bottom of the runway and took most of a day to get in the can. In between shooting Richard Riding had a long chat with Bentine, during which the accompanying photographs were taken. At the time Richard suffered migraine headaches and Bentine, a fellow sufferer, was able to give some useful advice. Bentine, who had been born at nearby Watford in 1922, also related some of his hilarious wartime experiences in the RAF, many of which became the subject of a radio series in later years. *(RTR)*

Shortly after the filming Elstree-based Fairchild Argus G-AIZE suffered a bad landing during which it shed its undercarriage and broke the propeller. No one was injured and the Argus can be seen today at RAF Cosford, restored to its former RAF colour scheme. *(RTR)*

As Hughie Green stepped out of his aircraft on landing at Elstree in about 1959 he walked up to Richard Riding and said, 'Good morning old son, where does one go for a pee in this place?' *(RTR)*

Racing driver Innes Ireland doing a bit of modelling at Elstree, c. 1963. His Beech 35 Bonanza G-ARZN can be seen in the background. *(RTR)*

Quite a change from old Hercules and the cart, and it would hold a lot of clobber! Harry H. Corbett and Wilfred Brambell, alias Steptoe and Son, pictured just before setting off from Elstree for the Biggin Hill Air Show in May 1964. *(RTR)*

14 Wolves in Sheep's Clothing

Since the war several private owners have acquired exotic military aircraft and based them at Elstree.

Tim Davies positions his Vickers-Supermarine Spitfire Type 361 IX G-ASJV/MH434 beneath the Piper Tri-Pacer cameraship 11,000ft over Essex during a flight from Elstree on 7 June 1964. *(RTR)*

Elstree's first privately-owned warbird was the Vickers-Supermarine Type 329 Spitfire II G-AHZI, named *Josephine*, owned by M.L. Bramson, a pre-war SE5A owner, who lived at nearby Kings Langley. Built at Castle Bromwich for the RAF as P8727 this Spitfire was first flown by Alex Henshaw on 16 June 1941. After the war P8727 was de-mobbed and sent to Marshalls of Cambridge, where it was fitted with a 1,440hp Rolls-Royce Merlin 45 and given a Certificate of Airworthiness on 22 October 1946. Sadly the black and cream Spitfire's stay at Elstree was short for on 15 April 1947 it crashed on take-off from Kastrup, Copenhagen and was written off. *(EJR)*

Between 1963 and 1967 Elstree was home to Vickers-Supermarine Type 361 Spitfire LF. IXC G-ASJV. Built at Castle Bromwich as MH434 for the RAF it was first flown on 8 August 1943 by Alex Henshaw. During service with No 222 (Natal) Squadron it destroyed at least two German aircraft. In 1947 the Spitfire was exported to the Royal Netherlands Air Force and served in the East Indies. Later the Spitfire passed to the Belgian Air force and was later transferred to COGEA at Ostend and used on target-towing duties bearing the civil registration OO-ARA. In June 1963 the Spitfire was purchased by Tim Davies and the aircraft was delivered to Stansted from Ostend on June 29 and flown to Elstree on 5 July 1963. *(RTR)*

Tim Davies flying his clipped-wing Vickers-Supermarine Spitfire IX G-ASJV from Elstree on 24 August 1963, two days after the aircraft's Certificate of Airworthiness was issued. Tips were added to the wings at a later date. *(RTR)*

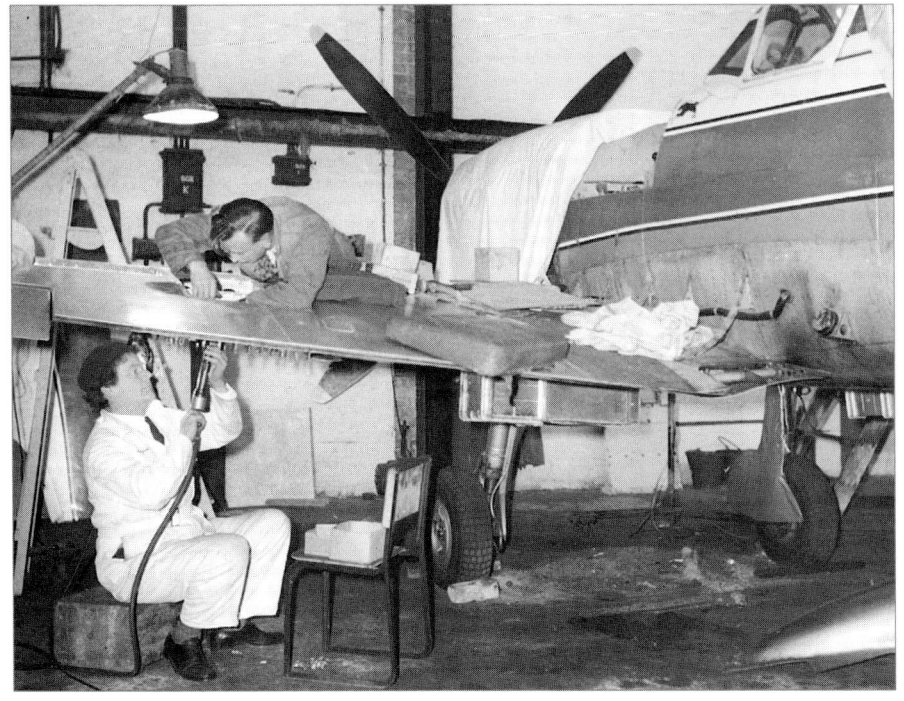

Fitting long-range wing tanks to Spitfire G-ASJV during the winter of 1964/5. Seen working on the aircraft are John 'Tubby' Simpson and a chap called Ted. *(RTR)*

After flying for a while with clipped wings Spitfire 'Juliet Victor's' elliptical tips were refitted, extra wing tanks were added and the aircraft had two 16mm cine-cameras mounted in the wings. Fitted with duplicated IFR radio equipment with transponder the owner regularly flew 'Juliet Victor' on airways. The aircraft was finished in white top surfaces, silver wings and lower fuselage with dark blue fuselage stripe and spinner. Final touches included a small black horse, the central motif of 222 Squadron's badge, reproduced beneath both sides of the windshield and the British Civil Air Ensign painted on the fin. Today the aircraft is owned and flown by the Old Flying Machine Company and based at Duxford. *(RTR)*

Preparing Spitfire 'JV for one of its many flights from Elstree. Bill Hallesey and his son Trevor were 'Juliet Victor's' unofficial ground crew and tended to her every need for four years. Bill is seen here using a bit of modern technology to secure the fuel cap on G-ASJV in about 1965. *(RTR)*

Young Trevor Hallesey watches as Tim Davies straps himself into G-ASJV. Note the rear-view mirror and the tool clipped into the inside of the hinged cockpit door, handy for breaking out of the cockpit in the event of an emergency. *(RTR)*

Below: As 'Juliet Victor's' 1,720hp Rolls-Royce Merlin 76 bursts into life Bill Hallesey and son Trevor prepare to move the trolley-ac away from the aircraft. *(RTR)*

Spitfire G-ASJV pictured 11,000ft over Essex during a flight from Elstree on 7 June 1964. *(RTR)*

A beautifully judged landing as Tim Davies brings Spitfire G-ASJV in for a three-pointer back at Elstree in 1964. Tim Davies bought G-ASJV for £2,000 in 1963 and sold it four year's later for £9,000. *(RTR)*

Shortly before Spitfire IX G-ASJV departed Elstree to become a star of the 1968 film *Battle of Britain* the two-seat Vickers-Supermarine Type 509 Spitfire Tr. 9 G-AVAV had moved in. G-AVAV was built at Castle Bromwich in 1943 as single-seat LF Mk IX MJ772 for the RAF. In 1950 it was converted into a two-seat trainer by Vickers and was sold to the Irish Air Corps in June 1951 and numbered 159. Retired from the Air Corps in 1960 it was acquired by Film Aviation Services and in 1966 was purchased by Tony Samuelson, one of the Samuelson film company brothers, whose company was based at nearby Cricklewood. Arriving at Elstree in bits on 3 January 1966 it was rebuilt by Simpsons Aeroservices and took to the air again in July 1967 in time to take part in the filming of *Battle of Britain*. In 1969 the aircraft was sold to Sir William Roberts and spent several years with the Strathallan Aircraft Collection until sold in 1974 to Doug Champlin who had the aircraft converted back to its original single-seat configuration. Here G-AVAV is seen undergoing undercarriage retraction tests at Elstree in 1967. *(RTR)*

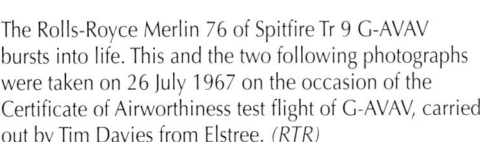

The Rolls-Royce Merlin 76 of Spitfire Tr 9 G-AVAV bursts into life. This and the two following photographs were taken on 26 July 1967 on the occasion of the Certificate of Airworthiness test flight of G-AVAV, carried out by Tim Davies from Elstree. *(RTR)*

Tim Davies taxies G-AVAV up the incline from the Elstree fuel pumps towards the taxiway. *(RTR)*

The moment of truth. Tim Davies turns G-AVAV into wind prior to taking off for the Spitfire's first post-restoration flight on 26 July 1967. *(RTR)*

John Schooling and Spitfire owner Tony Samuelson flying circuits and bumps in the Spitfire T.9, now camouflaged but still carrying its civil registration letters, at Elstree in 1967. *(RTR)*

With the sun slowly sinking in the west Tim Davies makes a perfect three-point landing in Spitfire G-AVAV at the conclusion of its 65-minute test flight on 26 July 1967. *(RTR)*

Above: Tony Samuelson's Hawker Hurricane Mk XII G-AWLW pictured at Elstree in 1968. Built by the Canadian Car and Foundry Company Ltd in Montreal this Hurricane flew with the Royal Canadian Air Force as 5588 and was later restored for R.E. Diemert at Manitoba and registered CF-SMI. The Hurricane arrived in Britain in 1967 and took part in the film *Battle of Britain*. In July 1968 it was registered to Tony Samuelson and taken to Elstree. On arrival at Elstree Simpsons Aeroservices pulled the Hurricane apart and it was awarded its first UK Certificate of Airworthiness in May 1969. The Hurricane is seen here in early 1969 during test running of the 1,635hp Rolls-Royce Merlin 25 engine. *(RTR)*

John 'Tubby' Simpson, his characteristic beret hiding an unruly shock of hair, with Hurricane owner Tony Samuelson discussing the intricacies of the Rolls-Royce Merlin 25 following an early engine run at Elstree in 1969. *(RTR)*

John Schooling taxiing out in Tony Samuelson's Hawker Hurricane G-AWLW for an air test one winter's day in 1969. *(RTR)*

John Schooling takes off for an air-test in Hawker Hurricane G-AWLW in 1969. G-AWLW was sold to W.J.D. Roberts at Shoreham in 1970 and after cancellation from the British civil register in April 1984 was acquired by the Canadian Warplane Heritage Museum and became C-GCWH/'P3069'. This rare aircraft was lost in a disastrous hangar fire at the Museum on 15 February 1993. *(RTR)*

Spencer Flack's two-seat Hawker Sea Fury T Mk 20S VX281, previously D-CACO in Germany, was registered G-BCOW in October 1974 and flown from Elstree in Fleet Air Arm colours by the owner. The Fury was sold to the USA in 1980 and currently flies as RN281 based at Santa Monica. *(RTR)*

Hawker Sea Fury FB XI WJ244, a former Fleet Requirement Unit aircraft, was acquired by Spencer Flack and registered G-FURY in July 1978. On 2 August 1981 engine problems forced Flack to crash-land short of the runway at RAF Waddington. The pilot was injured and the scarlet-painted Fury was written off.

Ray Hanna taxiing Spencer Flack's Supermarine Spitfire FR XIVe G-FIRE prior to the aircraft's first post-restoration flight at Elstree on 14 March 1981. Originally taken on RAF charge as NH904 in March 1945 the Spitfire was later supplied to the Belgian Air Force. Following ten years on the roof of a scrap yard near Ostend the wingless Spitfire was returned to the UK and mated with the wings of RM694. The Spitfire was sold to Sir William Roberts in 1971 and after being purchased by Spencer Flack in 1979 was carefully rebuilt. Though seen here in primer paint the Spitfire was later painted scarlet overall and joined the owner's similarly painted Hawker Hunter G-HUNT and Hawker Sea Fury G-FURY on the airshow circuit. *(Peter R. March)*

Ray Hanna three-points Spitfire G-FIRE on to Elstree's runway at the conclusion of its successful first post-restoration flight on 14 March 1981. *(Peter R. March)*

Former Danish Air Force Hawker Hunter Mk 51 E-418 was first flown in April 1956 and served with No. 724 Squadron until 1974. After the Hunter was returned to the UK in 1975 the airframe was acquired by Spencer Flack and removed to Elstree where it was restored to airworthy status. On 20 March 1980 Stefan Karwowski flew the Hunter out of Elstree to Cranfield. The Hunter duly appeared in overall red paint scheme and, registered G-HUNT, was displayed at many UK air shows. In September 1981 the Hunter was acquired by Mike Carlton and based at Hurn, Bournemouth. *(RTR Collection)*

Not strictly a warbird but part of the 'Elstree Air Force', according to the legend printed beneath the cockpit canopy. Pictured here at Elstree after its maiden flight on 1 December 1979 is the first WAR Aircraft Replicas half-scale Focke-Wulf 190 to fly outside the USA. Registered G-WULF and built and owned by Elstree-based S.B.V. Aero Services, the aircraft made a trouble-free maiden flight in the experienced hands of W.H. 'Bill' Bailey, who was responsible for all the initial test flying. The Fw 190 took 18 months to build, was fully aerobatic (+6g to -6g), and had a roll rate of 180 degrees per second and a maximum cruising speed of 145kt. The take-off and landing runs were both 700ft. Although the aircraft's basic airframe was of wood, polyurethane foam and fibreglass were extensively used. The undercarriage was fully retractable. G-WULF was still airworthy in 2003. *(RTR)*

15 Pulling the Crowds

Elstree flying displays have proved popular since the 1940s.

BOAC Short S.25 Sandringham 5 G-AHZE *Portsea* made a few low passes over Elstree during the air display of 27 July 1947. (*The Aeroplane*)

The cover of the souvenir programme for the 1947 Elstree Air Display featured a nice drawing of the aerodrome showing United Services Flying Club Auster Autocrat G-AGXJ passing overhead. The cost of the programme was 1s (5p) which was a bit steep considering that 12,000 visitors had already paid 3s (15p) for admission. In addition it cost £1 to park in the 'special aerodrome car enclosure'. The flying club must have spent most of the following week counting the takings! *(Via Michael Stroud)*

Another view of BOAC Short Sandringham G-AHZE *Portsea* making a low pass over Elstree during the air display of 27 July 1947. In the foreground is John Houlder's Miles Messenger G-AJOD. *(EJR)*

Described in the display programme for 27 July 1947 as the 'World Tramp of the Air' LAMS Handley Page Halifax G-AIWK *Port of Sydney* beat up Elstree several times before continuing on its way from Stansted to Milan loaded with freight! *(The Aeroplane)*

An aerial photograph taken during the air display on 27 July 1947, when 12,000 people turned up to watch the fun. In addition to the usual run of the mill de Havilland, Miles, Percival and Auster types a Heston Phoenix, Lockheed 12, Airspeed Consul and an Ercoupe can be seen in attendance. *(The Aeroplane)*

Duncan Simpson flying Hawker Aircraft's ancient 1931 Hart II G-ABMR/J9933 over Elstree reservoir on 18 June 1961 on the occasion of that year's Pilots' Rally. In 1972 the Hart was given to the RAF Museum at Hendon to form part of the Camm collection, where it is currently on display. *(RTR)*

An aerial view of the 40 or so aircraft that attend the Elstree Pilots' Rally on 18 June 1961, the two highlights being the presence of the Hawker Hart G-ABMR/J9933 and Vickers-Supermarine Spitfire Mk VB AB910 flown by Dave Morgan. *(RTR)*

Opposite: Programme cover for the 1979 Elstree Airshow featuring Spencer Flack's two-seat Hawker Fury and a motorcycle stunt that on the day went horribly wrong. Daredevil motor cyclist Robin Winter-Smith was attempting to leap across 32 Rolls-Royces but clipped the edge of the landing platform and was hurled into the steel scaffolding supporting the platform. He was killed instantly in front of a crowd of 10,000 spectators at Elstree on Sunday 8 July 1979. *(Rodney Saunders Collection)*

London School of Flying CFI David Greenland flying his Nord 1002 Pingouin G-ASTG at the 1966 Elstree air display on 4 June. Though recorded as being scrapped at Gatwick in 1970 the aircraft is currently at Duxford. *(RTR Collection)*

Below: Hawker Siddeley Dominie T.1 XS736, built at Chester in 1966 makes a touch-and-go at the Elstree Air Display held on 4 June that year. *(RTR)*

The cover of the programme for the 1967 Elstree Air Pageant. *(RTR Collection)*

Every private owner of a British-registered aircraft was invited by David Ogilvy to attend the Elstree Pilots' Rally, held on 19 July 1959, and 82 aircraft turned up. British aircraft; Miles, Auster, de Havilland and Percival types prevail, with not an American spamcan in sight! However, the advancing tide of all-metal, radio-equipped, nose-wheeled light aircraft from across the Atlantic was fast approaching and by 1960 American Cessna and Piper singles and twins began to set the trend for the next forty years. *(RTR)*

Significant Historical Events

Not Covered in the Original Edition

On 22 April 1946 a speed trial took place on the aerodrome's runway. A group of local motorists, co-ordinated by the Vintage Sports Car Club and the North London Enthusiasts' Club, petitioned the Air Ministry, who owned the site, to allow them to hold an event which would enable them to exercise their pre-war racing cars. With the support of the aerodrome, it was agreed that a speed trial could take place on Easter Monday. This would use the single runway in an east–west direction and time the competitors over a quarter of a mile, slightly uphill. They were to run in pairs, akin to modern-day drag racing, although they would be timed individually; there was also a knock-out element to the competition.

A larger than expected crowd of over 10,000 turned up and it took a while for the organisers to arrange them safely on the aerodrome grass. The fastest timed run was recorded by Peter Monkhouse driving a Bugatti Type 51, a classic pre-war sports car. He completed the quarter mile from a standing start in 15.2 seconds, crossing the finishing line at about 100mph. Although a success, the event was to remain a one-off, probably due to ongoing opposition from the Air Ministry. Credit was given to Fairfield Aviation and LAMS for use of the aerodrome and Watford hospital received a donation of £1,000.

Several long-distance flights started from the aerodrome in the post-war years:

- In October 1949 Barbara Duffy and Chris Gordon-Marshall flew to Nigeria in Auster 5 G-AKWH
- January/February 1957 saw Peter Jordan undertake a solo flight to Jos, northern Nigeria, in DH Tiger Moth G-ANZY
- In September/October 1964 Ken Vos flew solo to Darwin, Australia, in his Scintex Super Emeraude G-ASMV

After Dr Graham Humby, manager of LAMS, left the company following a serious medical issue, he immigrated to Australia for the sake of his health, where he revived his medical career and became a leading plastic surgeon. In 1934 he had invented the 'Humby Knife' used for taking skin grafts and a similar version is still in use today.

Events Since 2003

Nothing particularly significant occurred until February 2012 when John Houlder, the former aerodrome operator, died two weeks short of his 96th birthday. He was Britain's oldest registered pilot and stopped flying at the age of 94, having amassed over 10,000 hours, although he needed to be accompanied by a safety pilot for the last couple of years. He started flying lessons in a DH Tiger Moth at Brooklands in 1938 and quickly obtained his pilot's licence. He went on to acquire an instrument rating which he held for fifty-nine years. He was the only pilot authorised to fly his beloved Aero Commander G-AWOE due to the number of modifications he had made to it. In 1950 he was appointed by Lord Aldenham to run the aerodrome, a role he maintained until 2010, although he was still actively engaged on day-to-day management of the aerodrome until his death. He has been described as 'a one-man English aviation institution'.

The aerodrome is now owned and operated by Aldenham Aviation Ltd, following the 2022 incorporation of Aldenham Aviation LLP and Montclare Shipping Company. Lord Aldenham and his four children are directors of the company, with eldest siblings Jessica Allen-Back and Humphrey Gibbs as managing directors.

There were few changes in the infrastructure and resident businesses at Elstree during the last couple of decades of John Houlder's tenure, but there have been some key changes since the family took the business back in hand in 2012:

- Cabair, which ran the London School of Flying and had been resident at the aerodrome since 1971, ceased trading in 2012. Firecrest Aviation, another training organisation, followed suit three years later. This left Elstree with little to no fixed-wing training, but that has now changed. As well as Flight Training London, the Elstree-based fixed-wing training organisations are Air Academy, Fly Elstree, Flyers Flying School, MAK Aviation and Stars Fly. Piper PA28s and Cessna 152s and 172s are the types mostly used for training. Elstree Helicopters/Flying Pig, ICE Helicopters and Hilti Air provide training for rotary-wing aircraft.
- In April 2013 the 'new' control tower was brought into use, although strictly speaking it was the original 1960 one extended in height and re-clad.
- July 2015 saw the completion of alterations and extensions to the rear of the Second World War-vintage Super Robin hangars, which comprised a three-storey addition and painting inside and out. This facility is now known as the Elstree Aviation Centre and is currently occupied by ICE Helicopters, Atlas

Helicopters and other businesses, with the hangarage managed by Aldenham Aviation.
- In May 2019 a new hangar, known as the Hunsdon Hangar, was completed and is used by Hilti Air. This was the first new building to be constructed on the aerodrome since the Kinetic or Coseley hangar in 1969.
- Another new hangar was completed in January 2022, known as the Southeast Hangar. This facility is used by Flight Training London and Sloane Helicopters. Flight Training London has been the busiest fixed-wing training school since their move from Panshanger, and they have installed a certified ALSIM multi-engine flight simulator following relocation from their old premises at Elstree.
- The Coseley or Kinetic hangar (as it is now known) has been renovated and fitted with four portacabins for the relocation of maintenance company London Elstree Aviation (formerly Metair). The rare MAP 'R'-type hangar constructed during the Second World War is used by private fixed-wing aircraft and helicopters.

Today Elstree is known as London Elstree Aerodrome and is the only licensed aerodrome in Hertfordshire, where there used to be six in the 1960s. It is the nearest general aviation airfield to London's West End (12 miles/19km) and is run by Aldenham Aviation and the Gibbs family. The single licensed runway is the same length as it was in 2003, 651m, and is still orientated 08–26. Some 150 aircraft are based there, roughly the same as in 2003, although around forty of these are helicopters, which is a significant increase from 2003. There are approximately 50,000 annual movements, of which roughly a quarter are rotary wing, with fixed-wing training restricted to four aircraft in the circuit at any time.

In summer 2021 the family took the management of the on-site café back in hand, renaming it The Aerodrome Café and working closely with trusted catering partners to provide a strong offering to resident businesses, customers and visitors. In September 2022 a summer open day was held at Elstree, the first large public event since 1979, with over 2,500 attendees and many stall holders and activities present. The enthusiasm for aircraft, the aerodrome and all things aviation was very encouraging, and Elstree hopes to be able to host similar events every two years to allow more of the local community to enjoy the aerodrome.

With funding from the William Gibbs Trust and in partnership with the Air League, Elstree aerodrome launched a career-focused outreach programme in 2022 to inspire young people in and around Hertfordshire to consider a career in aviation. 'Soaring to Success' bridges the gap between education and industry, working alongside schools to showcase the range of opportunities within the sector through higher education and apprenticeships. In 2023 around 8,000 pupils were reached and the programme is now supported by Boeing, British Airways, the Department for Transport and the Civil Aviation Authority, who have helped expand the programme across the country.

While celebrating Elstree's past and present, it is vital to look to the future, and the aerodrome team is committed to preserving it as a popular hub for general aviation and innovation for many years to come. To provide a fantastic service to a wide range of aviation and commercial customers, there are always improvements that can be made to facilities and infrastructure that are vital to the operations of an aerodrome

– especially one that has been built up piecemeal since the war. The field is highly active but relatively small, so the team is looking at ways to improve the flow of fixed-wing, rotary and ground traffic, and enhancing the experience of pilots, passengers, thousands of annual visitors and the ops team. New technologies come and go – there is always exciting innovation in the industry – but it is not always easy to identify those which could suit a small general aviation airfield in the future. With any luck, there will be several opportunities for decarbonisation and quieter flight in the coming years. As with the last ninety-plus years, Elstree is a work in progress. Long may that continue!

The following photographs depict a variety of aircraft resident or visiting Elstree, as well as new buildings which have been constructed, since the original book was published in 2003. They are mostly courtesy of local photographer Mark Mockridge of nbalchemy (MM) and the remainder are by the author (GRP).

The 'new' control tower at Elstree pictured on 4 May 2023. It had been brought into use ten years earlier but, strictly speaking, it is the original 1960 tower extended in height and re-clad. *(MM)*

Above: This photograph, taken on 4 May 2023, shows the two new hangars constructed at Elstree in the last four years. The right-hand one, known as the Hunsdon Hangar, was completed in 2019 and is currently occupied by Hilti Air helicopters. On the left is the Southeast Hangar, built in 2022 and in use by Flight Training London and Sloane Helicopters, a major helicopter sales and maintenance organisation which has other bases at Sywell, Northolt and Enniskillen. *(MM)*

Rear view of the Second World War vintage Super Robin hangar on 22 May 2023 showing the substantial three-storey extension completed in 2015. This is known as the Elstree Aviation Centre and is currently occupied by ICE Helicopters, Atlas Helicopters and other businesses. *(GRP)*

Robinson R44 Cadet G-ICEZ belonging to Elstree-based ICE Helicopters was photographed on 16 September 2021. Robinson helicopters are very popular and over 13,000 have been built since the company was established in Torrance, California, in 1973. *(MM)*

Another Robinson product, R22 Beta G-FOLI, pictured here on 19 August 2019. It was transferred to Germany in April 2021. *(MM)*

Alpi Pioneer G-CEAR is an Italian-manufactured light sport aircraft, pictured here taking off from Elstree on 6 March 2020. There are currently more than fifty on the British civil register. *(MM)*

Tony Yarnold about to lift off from Elstree's runway 26 in American General AG-5B Tiger D-ENTO for a flight to Leeds East (Church Fenton) on 7 October 2020. The author is a regular passenger with Tony on flights around the country. 'Tango Oscar' has since been placed on the British register as G-ENTO. *(MM)*

Events Since 2003

Although American registered, this Beech E55 Baron N60526 is based at Elstree. It is pictured taking off from runway 26 on 31 May 2021 with its undercarriage doors not fully retracted. *(MM)*

Cessna 208B Grand Caravan G-UKPA, which visited Elstree on 14 July 2021, is used for parachute dropping from its home base at Sibson, Peterborough. *(MM)*

National Police Air Services' MBB BK117 G-DCPB operated for West Yorkshire Police visiting Elstree on 13 August 2021. *(MM)*

Eurocopter EC120B Colibri G-TGGR is based at Elstree and is seen here on 13 September 2020. *(MM)*

N445ML is a Cirrus SR22T, seen here taking off on 23 January 2023. This type of aircraft is a regular visitor to Elstree and several are based here. Over 9,000 SR20s and 22s have been built since 2001 at the company's plant at Duluth, Minnesota. *(MM)*

Van's RV9 G-ORVS visiting Elstree on 9 September 2021. Van's aircraft are mostly kit built and are extremely popular with the home-building fraternity. There are over 500 examples currently on the British civil register. *(MM)*

Elstree-based Robin DR400 G-SJBB taking off from runway 26 on 4 April 2022. Note the distinctive cranked wing which distinguishes most Robin & Jodel aircraft, also evident in the picture below. *(MM)*

1964-built Jodel DR1050 Sicile G-AWWO returning to its home base in Wiltshire on 3 August 2022. This aircraft is unusual in that its Continental engine has been replaced with a Rotax 912 which gives it improved performance and fuel economy. *(MM)*

Diamond DA42 Twin Star G-ZOLA departing runway 08 on 28 March 2022. This is one of many twin-engined aircraft based at Elstree. *(MM)*

Belgian-registered Cessna 182Q Skylane OO-COR photographed on 17 July 2021. This aircraft was transferred to the British register in May 2022 as G-FEEN and is currently based at Elstree. *(MM)*

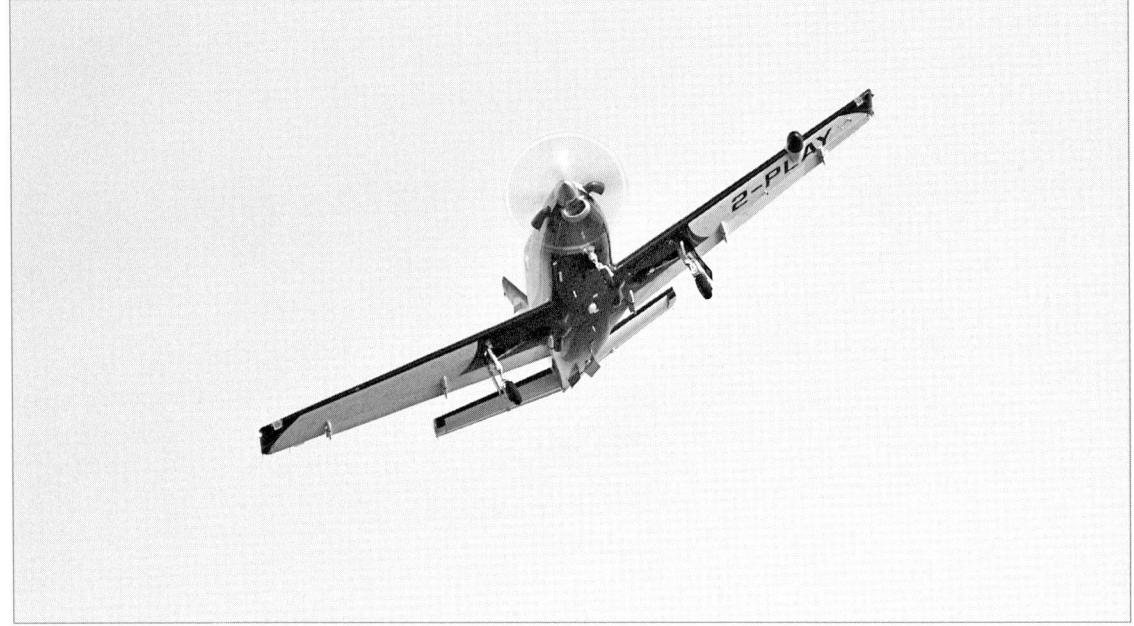

Guernsey-registered SOCATA TBM700 2-PLAY taking off from Elstree on 20 September 2021. It was exported to the USA as N302JG on 10 March 2022. *(MM)*

1960-built Piper PA22-150 Caribbean returning to its home base at White Waltham on 3 March 2022. *(MM)*

Formerly OK-AGT, this Piper PA28-161 Warrior was imported from the Czech Republic in 2012 and subsequently placed on the British register as G-OMCH. It is one of many PA28s based at Elstree and is currently used by Flyers Flying School for training. It is pictured here on 19 April 2021. *(MM)*

G-DTCP is a Piper PA32R-300 Lance based at Elstree, and is seen here departing runway 08 on 19 August 2022. The PA32 is a stretched version of the ubiquitous PA28 shown in the picture above and can normally accommodate two extra passengers. *(MM)*

Aerospatiale AS355 Ecureuil G-NLSE operated for Network Rail, pictured on 25 March 2022. *(MM)*

Westland Sea King G-SEAK masquerading as the President of the United States' *Marine 1* on a visit to Elstree on 18 June 2022. This aircraft was formerly XZ588 with the RAF when it was painted an overall yellow. *(MM)*

Bell 206B JetRanger G-NORK photographed on 17 April 2021. The popular JetRanger first flew in 1966 and more than 7,000 were built before production ceased in 2010. They were mostly manufactured at Bell's Mirabel plant in Quebec, Canada, and also under licence by Agusta in Italy as the AB206. *(MM)*

North Weald-based Agusta Westland AW169 G-HHEM operated by the Essex & Herts Air Ambulance service, on a visit in June 2021. Medevac and police helicopters are regular visitors to Elstree for refuelling. *(MM)*

This Agusta A109S Grand G-EMHE, pictured on 21 December 2021, was imported from Australia. *(MM)*

Pilatus PC12s are regular visitors to Elstree and at least one is based there. This Manx-registered example, M-SAXY, is seen here departing runway 26 on 10 June 2022. Whilst PC12s are somewhat big and heavy, they have no problems operating from Elstree's relatively short runway. *(MM)*

Mind the prop! This head-on view of an unknown PC12 was taken at Elstree on 10 September 2021. *(MM)*

Lithuanian-registered Yakovlev Yak 18T LY-CCP visiting Elstree on 24 March 2022. It is operated by Thommen Aircraft Equipment, a Swiss-based avionics manufacturer, and is a regular visitor to European airfields, including many in the UK. *(MM)*

Another Yakovlev product, silver YAK 50 G-YAKZ in Russian Air Force markings '33', photographed over Elstree on 20 September 2020. *(MM)*

Czech Aircraft Works CZAW SportCruiser G-ISCD photographed departing Elstree's runway 26 on 20 January 2020. Many SportCruisers are home built from kits and there are currently around 100 on the British register. *(MM)*

Events Since 2003

1948-built Cessna 195B N999MH is seen here on Elstree's runway on 13 April 2019. *(MM)*

This diminutive aircraft is an Avions Fairey Tipsy Nipper, appropriately registered G-NIPS. It was photographed on 18 January 2020, landing on runway 26 at Elstree. *(MM)*

I-RAIT is an Italian-registered Agusta Westland AW169, operated by Hoverfly, which was demonstrating its capabilities at Elstree on 4 May 2016. *(GRP)*

An unusual visitor to Elstree on 12 July 2019 was this float-equipped, German-registered Cessna U206 Stationair D-EBIW. It was built in 1995 and powered by a non-standard Rolls-Royce turbine engine. *(GRP)*

Aviat Husky G-CLIX is a two-seat utility aircraft built by Aviat Aircraft of Wyoming, as N12UK, in 2007. It was previously registered in Switzerland as HB-KHS and is seen here at Elstree on 9 September 2020. *(MM)*

A pair of Elstree based Guimbal Cabri G2s G-RJVH & G-FPEH hovering in the rotary wing manoeuvring area on 15 December 2020. These two seat light helicopters are built by Helicopteres Guimbal in France and first flew in 2005. *(MM)*

Piper PA38-112 Tomahawk G-BRHR was built in the USA in 1979, where it was first registered as N2377P. It has had multiple owners, including the locally based London School of Flying. It is currently used for training by Fly Elstree and is seen here on 18 January 2020. *(MM)*

G-ROFS is an Italian-designed Nando Groppo Trail two-seat light sport aircraft built in 2013. It is pictured here departing Elstree's runway 26 on 21 January 2020. *(MM)*

Events Since 2003 217

This 2005-built Beech A36 Bonanza N536EU was one of four previously on the strength of the Israeli Air Force and imported to Elstree in 2020. It was formerly 399 with the IAF and is pictured here on 20 May 2020. *(GRP)*

Black and yellow Aerospatiale AS355 Ecureuil G-NLDR visiting Elstree on 26 October 2020. *(MM)*

This Swiss-registered Klemm 35 HB-UBK was built in 1940 and it was en route from Southend to Old Warden when it force-landed in a field at South Mimms due to engine problems. Neither the pilot nor the passenger were injured and the remains were taken to Elstree, where it was photographed on 14 August 2016. It has since been repaired and is flying again. *(GRP)*

This smart Agusta Westland AW109SP GrandNew G-GALI was photographed on 16 July 2021. *(MM)*

Piper J3C-65 Cub G-BKHG is a Second World War veteran built in 1942. It is photographed here in USAAF markings as 479766 departing Elstree for its home base at Duxford on 11 May 2023. *(MM)*

This unusual visitor is Boeing Chinook HC6 ZK559 of No. 7 Squadron RAF, based at Odiham, Hampshire. It was carrying out tactical exercises on Elstree's runway on 29 September 2023. *(MM)*

The sad remains of John Houlder's beloved Aero Commander 680E G-AWOE in the 'graveyard' at Elstree in September 2023. John acquired this aircraft in 1968 and owned it for nearly forty-five years and was still flying it, albeit with a safety pilot until a couple of years before his death aged 95 in 2012. Compare this photo with the one on page 93, which shows 'Oscar Echo' in pristine condition just after delivery to Elstree. *(MM)*

Another Commander in a slightly better condition than the one previously pictured is 695A M-BETS, which was a regular visitor to Elstree until it was sold to the USA as N695DR in January 2023. It is pictured here departing runway 08 on 17 August 2019. *(MM)*

This view of the RAF's Battle of Britain Memorial Flight's Avro Lancaster PA474 flying over Elstree on 30 June 2019 evokes memories of a similar occasion when a four-engined bomber 'beat up' the aerodrome seventy-two years earlier. During an air display on 27 July 1947 a LAMS Handley Page Halifax loaded with fruit made several low passes over the runway en route from Stansted to Milan (see page 46). PA474 put in a further appearance over Elstree on 16 May 2023 to mark the 80th anniversary of the famous dams raids. It was on a tour of former RAF bomber bases and had just flown over the nearby RAF Museum. *(MM)*

Four single-engined members of the Battle of Britain Memorial Flight in formation over Elstree on 21 September 2020, comprising Supermarine Spitfires P7350, AB910 and TE311, and Hawker Hurricane LF363. *(MM)*

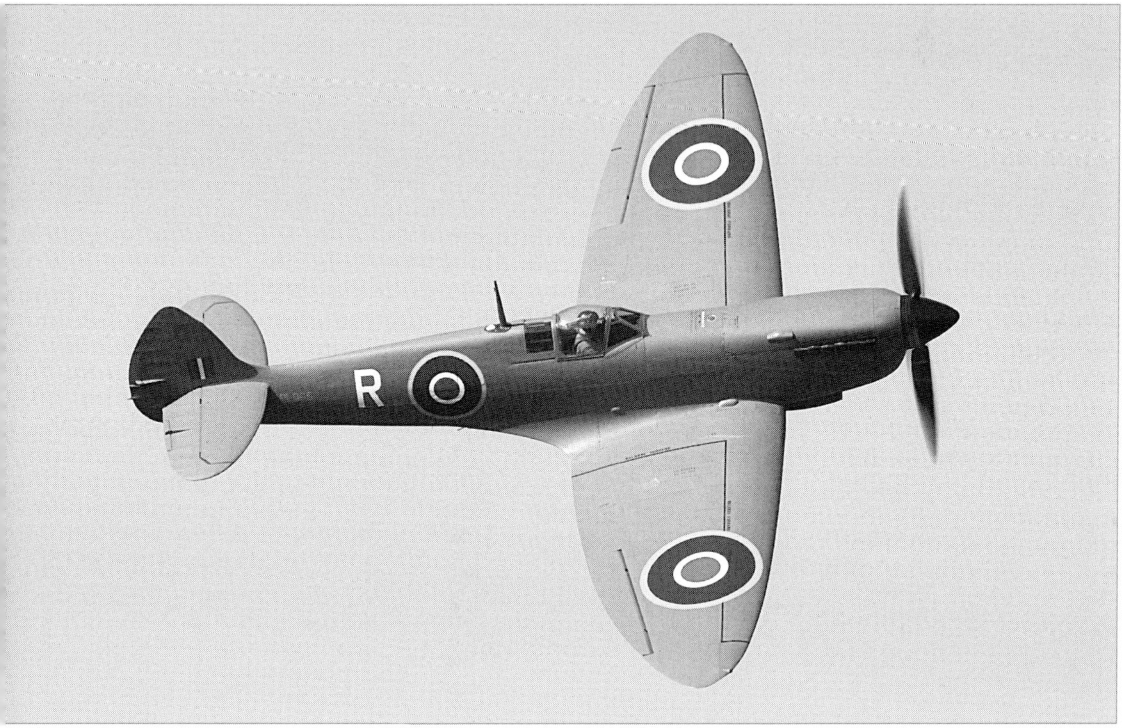

1944-built Vickers Supermarine Spitfire PRX1 PL965/G-MKXI pictured here in blue photo reconnaissance colours on 18 March 2022. It is owned by Peter Teichman and is part of his Hangar 11 collection of 'warbirds' based at North Weald. Peter commutes regularly to the Essex airfield from Elstree in his Beech Bonanza. *(MM)*

Two unidentified helicopters pictured departing Elstree on a shuttle service to the British F1 Grand Prix at Silverstone on 9 July 2023. *(MM)*

Czech-built Evector-Aerotechnik EV97 Eurostar G-CEVS is a light sport aircraft, seen here departing Elstree's runway 26 on 22 January 2023. *(MM)*

Events Since 2003   223

hree Elstree-based Piper PA28s returning from a fly out on 17 November 2023. They are apparently back-tracking from the
Charlie' hold, two having waited for the third to land. *(David Williams)*

iew of the highly successful Summer Open Day which took place on 1 September 2022. This was the first significant public event
 take place at Elstree since the airshow on 8 July 1979, which was marred by the death of a stunt motorcyclist (see pages 192–3).
his scene is similar to the one of the 1947 air display on page 191. *(MM)*

Sources & Acknowledgements

Air-Britain and the British Aviation Archaeological Council, *The Halifax File,* 1982
Avery, J.R., *The Story of Aldenham House,* 1961/96
Cramp, B.G., *British Midland Airways,* 1979
Hamlin, John, *Peaceful Fields, vol. 1 – A directory of civil airfields and landing grounds in the UK from 1919 to 1939,* 1996
Lane, John, *The Redwing Story,* 1992
Lawrence, A., *The Aldenham House Gardens,* 1988
Lovell, Mary S., *Straight on till Morning,* 1987
Markham, Beryl, *West with the Night,* 1942
Merton-Jones, A.C., *British Independent Airlines since 1946,* 1976/77
Ord-Hume, Arthur W.J.G., *On Home-Made Wings,* 1997
Ord-Hume, Arthur W.J.G., *British Light Aeroplanes,* 2000
Robertson, Bruce, *Lysander Special,* 1977
Sanders, Clarice, *Between Heaven and Earth,* 1997

Airfield Review (Airfield Research Group)
The Aeroplane
Flight
Popular Flying
Borehamwood & Elstree Times
The Barnet Press
The West Herts Post and *Watford Newsletter*
The Watford Observer
The Herts Advertiser and St Albans Times
Public Record Office files
Hertsmere Borough Council planning files

The authors gratefully acknowledge the valuable assistance given by the following:

Air Historical Branch, MOD; John Ausden; Fred Ballam, Hon. Archivist of Westland Aerospace; Civ Aviation Authority Registration Dept; Lettice Curtis; Timothy A. Davies; Denis M. Evans, flying instructo with No. 124 ATC Gliding School (1946–7); Former Fairfield Aviation employees Arthur Toms, Geoffre Davison, Reg Allory, Derek Higgs and Frank Barton; Haberdashers' Aske's School's Hon. Archivist; Th Handley Page Association; Hertfordshire Libraries and Record Office; John Houlder of Montclare Shippin Company, Aerodrome licensee and leaseholder; Philippa Martin and Jonathan Lane, children of John Lane Fairfield's Director and General Manager (1942–5); Roger T. Jackson; Stuart McKay; Michael Oakey an Nick Stroud of *Aeroplane;* David Ogilvy; David Oliver; Arthur W.J.G. Ord-Hume; RAF Museum, Dept o Research & Information Services; John 'Sandy' Sanders, Aldenham Aerodrome Manager (1937–9); Joh Schooling; Dave Smith; Michael Stroud; Brian Turpin; Lavinia Wellicome, Curator, Woburn Abbey.

Cover illustrations. Front, top: Four members of the Red Arrows overflying the aerodrome on 16 June 2019 'Red 1', Martin Pert, learnt to fly at Elstree having worked there as a plane-mad 16-year-old, pumping fue and moving aeroplanes. 'Elstree will forever hold a fond place in my memories,' says Martin. *(Cpl As Keates/MOD) Front, bottom:* San Marino-registered Agusta Westland AW139 T7-LSS pictured on 9 Jul 2023. San Marino is a tiny land-locked country in north-east Italy with a population of less than 34,000 bu has over 400 aircraft on its register. *(MM) Back:* Poster for the 2022 Summer Open Day.